"A thought-provokin[g]... able hero."
—*Kirkus Reviews*

"With its intrigue, discovery, problem-solving, and extraordinary encounters, Cicek Bricault has created an engaging story to attract STEAM learners. They will relish this captivating story of a girl who decides when to take risks and how to accept more responsibility as a leader.
—*Midwest Book Review*

"Readers will be glued to the sidelines cheering for KyRose. Supporting characters are original and well-defined, and the teens' dialogue and behavior are dead-on. The story carries a timely theme about the interconnectedness of all life and the importance of protecting our ecosystems and fellow creatures."
—*BlueInk Review*

"Like dogs, all animals have a unique intelligence based on their biology, each with so much to teach us. What a gift to young readers—as kids will absolutely delight in the escapades of KyRose and her fantastic array of classmates and furry friends while also expanding their perspective of the world."
—Tamar Geller, *New York Times* best-selling author of *The Loved Dog*

"KyRose...is a relatable heroine. She...makes decisions in haste, leading to teachable moments. Further, her discussions of echolocation, space exploration, and the intricacies of ecosystems are edifying. By the book's end...her family's history all unite in the emotional conclusion."
—*Forward* Clarion Reviews

This is a story that will inspire and delight middle-graders everywhere.
—Alan Watt, best-selling author of *The 90-Day Novel*

Kyrose Takes a Leap

Cicek Bricault

KYROSE PRESS

This is a work of fiction. Names, characters, places, and incidents either are the product of the author's imagination or, if real, are used fictitiously. Any resemblance to actual persons, living or dead, events, or locales is entirely coincidental.

KyRose Takes a Leap
Copyright © 2022 by Cicek Bricault
All rights reserved.

No part of this book may be used or reproduced, stored in a retrieval system, or transmitted in any form or by any means, electronic, mechanical, photocopying, recording, or otherwise, without the written permission of the publisher except in the case of brief quotations embodied in critical articles and reviews.

Published in Venice, California, U.S.A.
For information, please contact KyRose Press at
www.KyRoseLoves.com.

Educators and librarians, for a variety of teaching tools,
please visit us at www.KyRoseLoves.com

Library of Congress Control Number:
2022912902

ISBN: 978-0-578-38232-6 (paperback)
ISBN: 979-8-9865791-0-8 (eBook)
ISBN: 979-8-9865791-1-5 (audio, coming soon)

Cover and typography by Mariya Prytula
Chapter artwork by Melise Bricault
Copy editing by Jessica McKelden

Text for this book is set in Minion Pro.
First paperback edition, 2023
First eBook edition, 2023

For Melise and Sema

One

Hands Up

A tickle runs over my ankle.

Time slows.

I bend down, staring into the grasshopper's eyes. "What are you doing on this field? There's no food." I brush my hand over the prickly blades of plastic grass.

"Huh? I must have taken a wrong turn," the grasshopper says. She lifts her wings. That's how grasshoppers hear—through a tiny organ near the base of their hind legs.

Coach Hartley shouts orders for us, seventh-grade girls, to line up for jumping jacks.

I lean against the goal post. "You can't stay here. We're in the middle of P.E. You'll get crushed!" I look over, past the school building, onto the street where self-driving cars swerve around each other like synchronized swimmers. My eyes keep combing. "There!" I point to the cluster of oak trees opposite the bleachers. "Come on." I cup the grasshopper. She darts back and forth against my palms. "Don't worry," I whisper, "I'll keep you safe."

But still, she jimmies her head through a crack between my thumbs and wriggles her body free. Standing up on my knuckles, she whirls her antennae in a frenzy. "Look out...for yourself!" she shouts.

I pivot, spinning on my heels. A ball is zooming toward me, descending like a meteorite. Blocking the sun, the tree, everything!

The grasshopper leaps slow motion into the air.

I jump, too, hands held high. Bam!

"Nice catch, KyRose!" Cora Lee lifts her silver-rimmed scopes. Her jet-black eyes sparkle. Cora's my best friend; she has been since kindergarten.

"Thanks!" I smile, but when I look around, the grasshopper's gone.

Suddenly, a shriek of laughter booms from across the field. Cora slides her scopes back on. A blue light blinks behind the tinted lenses.

"Oh-oh!" Cora says, hands on her hips.

I squint. A darkened figure, silhouetted by the sun. Muscular and tall. Golden hair twirled in a bun. I recognize *her* immediately. Georgia Alister Schmidt, the most popular and ruthless girl at MakerX20, our middle school for seventh and eighth graders. It's been a grueling three weeks since we started school, and Georgia's already plucked her way to the top. Captain of the soccer team. She holds court at lunch every day, though she's never invited Cora or me to sit with her. Not yet, anyway. Only *Primas* are allowed. Handpicked by Georgia herself.

"OMG! She actually caught it!" Georgia hollers.

I freeze. Was that a compliment?

"Beginner's luck," Avery Mortedella shouts, tipping her hips. Strawberry-brown curls dance down her shoulders, and a giant bow with polka dots crowns her head. Avery is a Prima, and follows Georgia around everywhere like a puppy dog. "Kick her another," Avery calls out. "Bet little Snow White won't get it. You know *that* girl thinks she can *talk* to animals." Avery laughs. Her words rocket through the air, slicing through me like shattered glass. I'm so sick of kids making fun of me because I'm different. My skin is brown anyway, not white like snow, and my last name is Sanchez, but that's not what matters. It's that other kids don't talk to animals like I do.

"Okay! Show me what you got!" Georgia shouts.

I gasp. It's the first time she's spoken to me ever. Her tone is serious, packed with warning. Tabeen Evli and Rebecca Johnson—the two other Primas in their tight-knit tribe—flock to Georgia's side. Tabeen's headscarf flaps in the wind, and Rebecca's skin glistens like an ebony angel under the sun. The two girls crane their necks in what must be snickering at me. Avery tosses the ball to Georgia, who kicks it high.

"You can do this!" Cora urges in a hushed and desperate cheer.

My feet shuffle side to side as my mind calculates the arc of the sphere heading toward me—a dazzle of black and white spinning like Yin and Yang. Have I misjudged? Will I make it? I reach my hands to the sky...to the invisible stars and moon. With all my might, I jump, wishing I were a gazelle…or a grasshopper.

"Got it!" I crash to the ground.

Before I can blink, Georgia's leaning over me.

"Woohoo! You got good instincts, *Keee-Rose*," Georgia says in a twang that clanks of confidence and grit.

Lost in her steel-gray eyes, I forget that she's mispronounced my name. Georgia offers me a hand. Her grip is strong, like a shark, and I wonder what kind of meal I'll be for her. I look to Cora, who nods, but not at me. She's busy scanning Georgia, taking in bits and bytes of "augmented reality" that only Cora can see projected through her scopes—which spit out digital blurbs like the brand of Georgia's charcoal eyeliner and her sparkly, pink blush, and another blurb, for sure, that touts Georgia's whopping 2,812 followers on FriendZ. What a far cry from my dismal number of three.

Avery, Tabeen, and Rebecca run over and crowd around us. Georgia puts her arm around me and smiles. I smell the sweet apricot scent of her hair conditioner, mixed in with her sweat.

"Don't let her fool you." Avery furls her brow. "She's no soccer player!"

A chill runs down my spine. She's right! When I was eight years old, Mom signed me up for junior soccer league at the rec center. I begged her everyday to let me go hiking with Abuela instead. I wanted to run in the wild fields and play with bunnies and badgers, not kick a stupid ball around. So, of course, without much practice, I never got good at soccer.

"We need a goalie for our team!" Georgia thunders. She squeezes my shoulder tight. The ground beneath me spins. Could she be serious? Me? Goalie?

"Our first game is next Tuesday. And we have to win!" Georgia narrows her eyes. "We play those jerks, the Victorians." She turns and looks me right in the eye. "Yeah, you need practice. But I know talent when I see it. You'll do fine."

"Really?" I mutter. Butterflies bounce in my stomach. Of course, Dad would say it's the microbes. I take a deep breath and try to be chill. I dust off my yellow, mylar gym shorts. So what if the fabric never gets dirty, and Mom bought me six pairs anyway 'cause she was in a rush, as usual?

Georgia holds her stare, waiting for me to say something like yippie. But I can't.

Beside us, Tabeen futzes with the knot that holds up her shirt.

Rebecca then leans in. Her beaded braids jangle like a drum roll. "Soooo. Whaddya think?" she sings in a voice that's inviting, like the sparrows outside my window at springtime.

But what if I fail? Georgia will kill me. I look at Cora in a silent plea for help. She gets it—as best friends do—and steps forward, hands on her hips once again.

"Maybe KyRose doesn't want to join the team?" Cora says. "Don't be a bully, Georgia!"

"No one asked your opinion, Coralina," Georgia snaps, hovering three inches taller than her.

But Cora doesn't back down. "You'll do anything to get what you want, won't you?"

Cora and Georgia inch closer. I tug and twist at my hair. My chest pounds. It's like a bomb is about to go off. Tick, tick, tick.

Finally, my voice cracks, "Pleazzze. Don't fight."

"Good. So, you'll be goalie!" Georgia smiles smugly and crosses her arms to seal the deal.

I shrug. What else could I say? Cora wrinkles her nose.

Georgia then calls Coach Hartley over. A fit woman in her mid-thirties, Coach has cropped hair dyed in patches of orange and black, same colors as our school mascot, the Jaguar. Across her gray tee is a silk-screened image of the cat that prowls across her bosom as she walks over.

"What's going on here?" Coach asks. Her voice is tough, no-nonsense. But when Georgia tells her the news, Coach warms up instantly. "Welcome to the team, KyRose Sanchez," she says, patting me on the back. "I'm sure our captain here will take good care of you. Right, Georgia? Nice recruiting, by the way!"

Georgia nods and stands tall. Well, tall-er.

The four Primas run off to do their jumping jacks. Then Coach pulls Cora aside.

"You know the rules," she says, pointing at Cora's scopes. "No tech on the field! That's *cheating*. If this were a game, we'd be kicked out of the league."

"Oops," Cora says, and pulls the lenses off her face. She winces in the bright sun. "I was, well, just testing them out for my mom's new company." Cora's mom is a serial entrepreneur. She started a bunch of tech companies, and now she invests in other people's ideas too. So Cora always gets the best gear. "They're still in beta," Cora says.

"I don't care what they're in," Coach snaps. "If I see 'em again, you'll be in the principal's office. Got it?!" She blows her whistle. P.E. is over.

As Cora and I head to the locker room, I turn back at the field and think of the grasshopper. I hope she made it to the trees without getting trampled on. I wonder if I'll be as lucky?

Two

Ready, Set, Go

Back in my comfy carbon jeans and loose khaki tee—that I bought from the pre-loved, thrift shop—I walk the halls of MakerX20. The X stands for infinite possibilities. Whatever that means. And the 20, well, that's for everything that came after the pandemic that swept the world in 2020. Back then, I was in diapers (pull-ups, actually), but I remember the daisy-print masks that Abuela sewed us out of her pillowcases. Mom and Dad said that schools changed big-time after the pandemic. They had to teach kids to be creators and solve the world's problems. Solve them when we get older, that is.

As I walk down the hall, kids pour out of classrooms—from robotics to coding, studio arts, game design, storytelling, engineering, and my favorite, life science. I watch as Georgia and Avery cruise by, arm in arm, wearing matching parachute pants. I wave, but they don't notice me now that P.E. is over.

"Hey, check it out," Rex Ramirez calls out. His hair is spiked and dyed neon green today. Whatever suits his mood and dazzles his followers. He's got over 20,000 of them. You see, Rex is a streamer, a content creator. He interviews everyone, including himself. I dodge around him and the black glove on his right hand. With it, he controls a mini-drone shaped like a giant beetle that zips back-and-forth over his head. With no teachers around, Rex boasts into the camera on his digi-bracelet. "Hey everyone, check out this drone. I made it myself. And, go on! Rank this maneuver!" He wriggles his fingers and sends the beetle into a double loop.

Dante Roberts comes jogging down the hall. His long bangs, swooped around his doll face, flop over his eyes as he runs. Dante yells, "Oh no! It's gonna cr-a-sh!" and swats. His scrawny twin brother, Dillon, ducks just in time. The beetle slams against the wall, breaking into pieces.

"Jerk!" Rex yelps.

And Ouch! I cringe. What if that were a real beetle?

The twins keel over, laughing. I've known them since second grade. They were monsters back then too, stomping on spiders, pouring glue over ants. Not much has changed.

Rex peers at his digi-bracelet. "Hold up! My viewers actually *liked* that!" He cheers, "Way to go!" and bumps shoulders with the twins.

I tug my Camp Catalina cap down over my sun-kissed brown hair and scurry to my locker. Thumb on the trackpad, it clicks open. Stomach rumbling, I rummage through my JellyGlobe backpack. From behind the solar flaps, I grab another of Dad's new snack bars. I tear the purple wrapper and take a bite. Crunchy millet and pink banana with a swirl of cocoa icing. Not bad. I can give him an honest "like" on his channel for this one. My mind wanders. I trace the edges of my sketchpad, a present from Abuela, for my twelfth birthday last January. That was before she got sick. Then, over the summer when I was at sleepaway camp on Catalina Island, she got worse. She cam'd me on the holocam and told me she had to leave for Ecuador the next day. Before it was too late, she had to get to the tiny village where she'd been born. "To be with our healers," she said. The Equilibrar natives live at edge of the Amazon Rainforest. She used to tell me stories about their magical ways. Before we hung up, she said, "Whatever happens, I'll always be with you…in here." She tapped her heart. "And remember. Always help the animals. Because if you don't, the universe might take your gift away."

I wonder if I'm going to ever see Abuela again. I miss her so much.

Whack! The locker door smacks into my arm.

"Oh…ah, sorry. You okay?" a voice mumbles. It's Will, my lab partner.

"Yeah. I'm fine." I rub my arm.

"Oh no! I bent your locker. Let me fix that," Will says, and pulls a toolset from his pocket. He throws a quick look over his shoulder. Dante is staring back at us and tips his chin.

"I'd stay away from him," I say.

"Who? That fool? He doesn't scare me," Will says, but his fingers fumble as he grips the pliers. Will flips his short bangs, and for a second, he looks like all the other California boys. But he's not. I heard him tell Ms. A, our science teacher, that he moved here this summer from some lake town outside of Chicago.

"All fixed!" Will smiles, but his deep blue eyes seem sad. Maybe he misses his friends back home?

"Thanks," I say, still rubbing my arm.

"See you in class," Will says, and walks off ahead of me.

I toss the wrapper from Dad's snack bar into The Recycler. The machine gobbles it up and hums as it melts the mixed plastic. Later, it'll get shaped into spools of filament. We use that in our 3D printers, mostly to make prototypes for our school projects.

As I keep walking down the hall, a slideshow plays on the wall with pictures of inventions that changed the world, like the wheel and the windmill. There's a printing press, a computer chip, a robot wearing scrubs performing surgery on a patient, and self-driving cars, trucks, and airplanes. Past the slideshow, in cherry red lights, the number "61" blinks. It's a countdown to the number of days until the landing of the first manned mission to Mars. The spacecraft *Mission Colonia* is plunging through space, with astronauts on board, ready to make history!

I turn the corner. A cool draft from an open skylight sways a banner that hangs from the ceiling. "Go Jaguars" dissolves into "Team Spirit!" By the trophy case, my knees wobble. I scan the gold and silver trophies, but there's nothing for seventh-grade girls' soccer. Now I get it! Georgia wants to make history! She wants to win the championship.

My mind drifts…I see her holding a great big trophy in her arms. "KyRose, we couldn't have won this without you," Georgia says. "Party at my house! Come on. You're the guest of honor!" She puts her arm around me, and we giggle.

The bell rings. I jolt from the daydream. I look around. I'm alone in the hall. But then a bumblebee zips past my nose. I follow him to the next trophy case over. Inside are plaques and ribbons for winners of science fairs and hackathons. The bee lands on the glass under a beam of sunlight.

"Hi there," I say, and gently I stroke his furry bands of yellow and black.

"You're not afraid of me! You're not like the other kids?" the bee asks, surprised.

"I'm a friend," I say. "Why ever would you sting me?"

"Only to protect my hive. I'd die for them." He spreads his wings, soaking in the warm light. Inside the case, below the bee, a tarnished plaque catches the sun. In the glimmer of the light, I make out the faded inscription. It reads:

Francis Maloney
Winner of the Inventables Contest
for his Electromagnetic Field Generator

The second bell rings. Dang! I'm late. Again! Ms. A's going to kill me. I start running and see a quote—they're written in black cursive all over the walls at MakerX20. This one is from Benjamin Franklin, the inventor that tied a metal key onto a kite, flew it in a storm, and discovered that lightning is, well, made of electricity. He also invented bifocals. Abuela always wore a pair on the bridge of her nose when she wrote her letters. Ben's quote here reads:

"Energy and persistence conquer all things."

Huh? All things, as in *anything*? Like if I try hard enough, Georgia will like me! Right, ol' Ben?

After school, I catch up with Cora as she unlocks her bike.

"So, you definitely joining the team?" she asks.

"Yeah."

"I thought you hated soccer." She looks at me and frowns.

"Yeah, but I can be friends with Georgia." I bounce on my toes. "Hey, I know. Why don't you join the team too?"

"What, so we can *both* kiss up to that brute and be…" Cora lifts two fingers and scrunches them into air quotes, "popular? No thanks!"

"Yeah, but we'll get invited to her next party!" I say. She had one last weekend. Of course, Cora and I weren't invited. But, I overheard Tabeen and Rebecca yammering on about how it was the best time ever.

Cora shrugs. "You know, I'm not into all that social party stuff. Too much drama! I'd rather be coding or hanging out with just you."

Just me? This is middle school, I want to scream. We have to blend in. "Pleazzze, join the team with me!"

"Nope!" Cora swings her bangs. "But don't worry. I'll cheer for you from the stands. Anyway, it's *you* they want." She sits up on her bike.

"But what if I mess up?" I let out a nervous giggle.

"You'll get up and try again. You'll be fine. Even if…oh, never mind." Cora waves her hand in the air.

A pit instantly gnaws in my stomach. "What? If it has to do with Georgia, you better tell me right now."

Cora looks at me square in the eye. "Okay. So, I kinda I hacked into Georgia's FriendZ account."

"You did what?!"

"Hey, it's all public information. You just need to know where to look—and how to decode it. I saw your friend request to her, by the way."

I shrug, guilty. Georgia never accepted it.

"Anyway, I read all her DMs," Cora says, referring to direct messages. "There's a girl named Marta. I guess they use to play club soccer together. Well, Marta was bragging on and on about how Georgia got pushed off the team 'cause she wasn't, well, good enough, if you can believe that. Georgia finally blocked her, but, I guess…you should know…Marta plays for the Victorians."

"You mean the school team we play next week!?"

"Yep."

"OMG. So, Georgia's gonna be out for blood. That's just great!" I roll my eyes.

"Don't worry. Just be yourself."

"Easy for you to say…from up in the stands."

Cora forces a smile and cruises off.

I scan the jacaranda tree for Skinner. I could use a hug right about now. But my favorite squirrel is nowhere in sight.

A swarm of kids run by. They jump onto five of the six MagBoard scooters parked along the sidewalk. I tap my digi-bracelet and unlock the last one. The MagBoard—which has no wheels—levitates three inches off the ground. The path beneath it is paved with tiny magnets. I give the board a push and *voila*! Off I go.

Three

Gotta Look Good

Riding home on the MagBoard, I cross six lanes of traffic and swoop into my neighborhood, Venice Beach. The air is balmy and smells of salt. The streets begin to narrow and are lined with cube-shaped homes scrunched together. Sandwiched between them is the occasional old bungalow. Hard to imagine, over a hundred years ago, all this was marshy wetlands with a giant lagoon in the middle, home to millions of seabirds. What a party that must have been! Colonies of cranes and gulls squawking and nesting. Sadly, they got pushed out by the miners who came to drill and pump oil out of the ground. California has tons of oil, even under the ocean floor off its coastline.

    I lean on the MagBoard and turn onto Driftwood

Avenue. There's a mural painted on the side of the old post office. It's of Abbot Kinney, with his pointy beard, wearing a top hat and blazer. He was the land developer who came after the miners and bought up the rest of the wetlands. Abbott Kinney had the crazy idea to build an amusement park here, a kind of Coney Island of the Pacific. Canals were dug and the wetlands drained to make the place look like Venice, Italy. That's how we got our name—Venice Beach. Abbott Kinney brought gondolas over from Italy to give people rides through the canals. He had a pier built with a giant rollercoaster, dance clubs, and a boardwalk filled with jugglers and musicians playing guitars and tambourines. He then built rows of bungalows and sold them to city folk who flocked here during the summer months to frolic by the beach. Years later, when the big pier burned down, Venice lost its luster. Later, it was reborn as an artist colony, and now it's a tech hub. Surfers and skateboarders cruise round everywhere. Dad l-o-v-e-s catching waves, though he's been too busy lately, opening his newest juice shop. And my brother, Jack, well, he pretty much lives at the skatepark. I guess I can see why Abuela fell in love with this place. She must have sensed the free spirit of those birds who lived here long ago.

Today many of the famed canals are gone, though a few still remain, linked to the marina—where on the other side, the City of Los Angeles established an official wetlands reserve for the wild part still left. And, around my neighborhood, the bungalows are ancient relics of the past. I ride by one now and hear a cat meow.

I slow the MagBoard and stop in front of a crooked picket fence. It wraps around a wobbly, wooden, two-story bungalow with blue paint chipping from its sides. In the center of the garden is a knobby, thick tree that keeps watch. Its canopy reaches wide and casts a shadow over its roots, which snake along the ground. Patches of wispy grass and purple wildflowers blanket everything in between. The garden is old, but smells wet and alive.

"Meow." Up in the tree, a caramel-colored kitty stands perched on a branch.

"Oh, are you stuck?" I ask. No collar around its tiny neck. No bowl of food or water left out on the porch. She must be feral with no one to take care of her. "It's okay, I'll help you down," I say.

"I'm outside and free. I like it here!" The kitty stands proud. At the other end of the branch on which she stands, a screen dangles from an open window. So, she must live here. I step off the MagBoard and tap my digi-bracelet and record a couple seconds of the kitty for my sketchbook. I then open the gate and carefully tiptoe into the garden, just in case the owner comes out yelling. But no one seems to be home. The kitty moves her gaze onto the next branch over, where a bundle of twigs are woven tightly together. She then crinkles her whiskers and hunches low ready to lunge. Suddenly, a pair of blue jays torpedo down from a tall palm tree.

"Stop that!" they squawk.

The kitty paws frantically trying to push the jays away, but she loses her footing. I leap, stumbling over the roots and catch her in my arms.

She whimpers.

"Are you okay?" I ask, rocking her back and forth like a baby doll.

Her amber eyes glow softly. "Ah, yeah...I think so. Thank you." She meows. "You-you saved my life."

My heart warms.

"I just want to be outside and make friends."

"I know. Me too. But you have to be careful," I say. "There could be eggs in that nest. And blue jays, like most animals, will do anything to protect their young."

"That's right! Tell her to watch it!" the mother jay chirps from above.

I kiss the kitty on her nose. She purrs. When I set her on the porch, I ask the jays to leave her be. I think she's learned her lesson. The kitty nods so cute, I can't resist. I want to share my joy. Before getting back on the MagBoard, I record three more seconds of video, then post it on FriendZ, #CutestKittyEver.

At the corner of 4th and Speedway, I come to a swooshing halt. My digi-bracelet zings. I tap and a FriendZ hologram plays over my wrist.

It's Georgia. She accepted my friend request! And, added a bunch of hearts on my kitty post! I practically fall off the MagBoard. In the comments, she writes, "OMG. Your brother is rana_sk8r! I had no idea. That's so cool!"

Twelve more FriendZ requests flood onto my screen. Friends of Georgia, or friends-of-friends of hers. Quickly, I park the MagBoard and accept them all, then skip the rest of way home. I strike the air with a swift kick. Ready to practice. Ready to win!

At my front door, a button-size camera scans my face. The door swings open and Alfred plods over. That's our robot. A couple inches shorter than me, Alfred's head, limbs, and torso are covered in white enamel. Its neck and joints (shoulders, elbows, wrists, hips, knees, and ankles) are trimmed in orange rubber. Alfred's eyes glow blue. Dad bought the robot when Abuela got sick. It was meant to be a nurse for her (and came with a twelve-month return policy). But, when Abuela left, Alfred needed a new job quick or Dad would send him back. Mom was all too eager to train him to be our butler.

"Welcome home. Let me get that for you, Ms.

KyRose," Alfred says all chipper as he takes my JellyGlobe backpack. Alfred speaks in a British accent, Mom's favorite setting. She says it reminds of her of TV shows she used to watch as a kid. In them, the butler would always walk in with tea and cucumber sandwiches on a silver platter. I guess Mom never got pampered like that. Probably because her mom died when she was young, but she doesn't really ever talk about that.

As Alfred hangs my backpack on a hook by the door, I ask, "Where's Mom?" I can't wait. She's going to be over the moon when I tell her I'm on the soccer team.

"Your mum's twenty-four minutes away in ShareCar #5." That's the car club we belong to now that Mom gave up driving over a year ago. She said why bother driving when a computer can do it better?

"What about Puddles?" I ask. He usually runs over when I get home. I look up the stairs and peek around the living room.

"The dog's at the groomers," Alfred says.

My heart sinks. Darn! I want to share my news with *somebody* around here. Guess I'll have to wait. I slip off my canvas sneakers that are stained with red clay from Camp Catalina, even though Alfred's washed them like twelve times. The robot wipes a finger across the entryway table, no doubt checking for dust. Its eyes blink rapidly with alarm. Maybe because of all those threats Dad's made to send him back the factory. I mean, how many cucumber sandwiches can Mom actually eat anyway? Plus, she's always out at work.

I tell Alfred the house looks great, very orderly.

"You think so?"

"Sure," I say.

His eyes grow steady and calm.

Just then, my nose catches a familiar scent. Fresh cut grass. I bounce straight to the kitchen.

"Dad! You're home?! Guess what?"

Standing over the sink with his back turned, Dad lifts a finger that's dripping wet, signaling for me to wait. "Be sure to wash the vegetables thoroughly," he says, addressing one of the three mini-cams flying around his head. Dad swishes his hands in the sink. His wavy, raven black hair is pulled back in a tiny bun like it usually is when he's preparing food. Draped around his lean body is his rubber apron with his brand, "Gut Love Foods," stamped across it.

I take a seat at the kitchen island. As I wait, my eyes dart to my bracelet. Nothing more from Georgia. So I scroll through my newsfeed, stopping at the headline, "Dolphin Rescued." I tap the eight-second clip. In it, two fishermen, one young with dark brown hair and other old with gray hair, haul a dolphin wrapped in blankets off a boat. "Pops and I had no idea the thing was tangled in our nets," the younger fisherman says as he rubs his pocket. He looks somewhat familiar to me. A rescue truck then drives the dolphin off, sirens blaring.

When the clip ends, I play it again and zoom in on the name of the boat: *Maiden Voyage*. Now I remember. That's the boat that was moored at the bottom of the cliffs on Catalina Island when I was there for camp this summer. It's the boat that brought that biologist named Troy, who used our camp as a base station to do his research on…what did he call it again? A *mysterious migration*. Troy was tagging fish, sea turtles, dolphins, and all kinds of seabirds, marking them with GPS tattoo trackers. I volunteered to help, and got to hold a bald eagle in my arms as he tattooed her neck. The eagle's name was Gabriella and I remember her mate Merlin sat perched up on a Toyon tree complaining the whole time, "You better not hurt her."

I play the clip once more. Yep, that's definitely Troy's friend—I think his name was Frankie. I say a prayer for the dolphin. Hope she's okay.

Finally, Dad peels off his gloves and calls, "Cut!" The cameras hover a second longer, then flit to their charging stations on top of the fridge.

"Ah, mi amor." Dad kisses my cheek. "I have to get this video out. You know how fickle my followers get." He winks.

Just then, my bracelet zings again. Another FriendZ request. Delighted, I smile and tap accept. But then I rub my wrist and wonder…what the heck I'm going to do to keep *my* followers happy?

Dad keeps prepping and waves his hand over a sensor on the side of the kitchen island. A cubby slides up. Inside is a conveyor belt that rotates his gadgets. A toaster, a blender, dehydrator, spectrometer, and more. They go around like a Ferris wheel. And, there's my favorite: a 3D printer that makes the best chocolate chip cookies in the world. Dad waves his hand again. The belt stops. He grabs a pistol-shaped juicer and places it on the counter beside me. He then turns around to the row of shelves on the wall by the fridge. Swinging his arms like an octopus, he grabs bottles of turmeric, powdered kale, and kelp. Each of the shelves are lined with potions. Jars, big and small, stuffed with delicacies like pink salt from the Himalayas and black salt from Hawaii, red spice from India, and wild cacao from Brazil. One entire shelf is devoted to ancient grains—teff, millet, quinoa—soaking in vats of water to "relax" so they'll be easier to digest. From the next shelf up, Dad grabs a bottle of kimchi bubbling with probiotics. The concoction, a Korean favorite, is made of cabbage, radishes, peppers, and ginger with just a touch of sweet rice vinegar. It ferments for days, growing lactic acid and bacteria. Dad pries the jar open, dips his finger and gives a lick. "Ah, tangy! But needs a few more hours." He slaps the jar back onto the shelf.

I know what you're thinking: *yuck*! But these are really healthy. They're Dad's secret ingredients. It's what his brand, Gut Love Foods!, is all about. He slips them into all his dishes, smoothies, and juices—especially the probiotics because they're living bacteria. Swallow that down the hatch and it feeds the trillion other microbes—itsy-bitsy organisms—that live in our tummies. Gut Love Foods! Get it?

Dad plops a handful of the greens from the sink onto a dish towel. The stalks are hairy and plump.

"Looks like it came from the bottom of the sea," I say, taking a sniff. A hint of salt runs over my tongue.

"Succulent ice plants! I just picked 'em off our roof today," Dad says. That's where Dad cultivates his greatest treasures: his seeds. Collected through a network of farmers from around the world, Dad plants the seeds in just the right season. After growing a sample—once he decides if he's going to use them in a recipe—he sends the seeds off to farmers outside the city, so they can grow a bigger yield. But first, he needs the recipe. Juiced, rolled, or dried?

"You ready to be my guinea pig?" Dad asks.

"Hey!" I fold my arms. "I thought you were against animal testing!"

"Of course. Vegan all the way!" Dad says, standing

proud. Me too. I can't bear eating animals. Not even eggs, milk, or honey. Nothing harvested from an animal. Like Dad, I only eat plant-based food. "Pero, mi amor," he says, "I don't think of you as an animal. You're my little girl."

"Little? I'm almost thirteen! And, guess what happened to *me* today?" I say, scooting his finger off the blender. I begin my story with the grasshopper and get as far as catching the first ball when Mom walks into the kitchen.

"You won't believe it." She sighs and kicks off her heels and drops her briefcase. Alfred catches it before it hits the floor. In front of the microwave door, Mom pats her hair. "Guess who had to go to the permit office? Again! All the way downtown. That's got to be my thousandth time. Demolition on Oyster Village starts next week. I swear, if the permits get delayed again, Mr. Sphinx is gonna *fire* me!" Mom plops onto a stool beside me. She gives me a tired smile.

"Oh, mi vida, you'll work your magic," Dad says to her.

"*Magic*? There's no such thing. Only hard work…and maybe a bribe or two." Mom's eyebrows lift and her emerald eyes sparkle as though she's up to something. "That inspector in the permit office? He loved your cookies, honey. Might be enough to pull some strings." She blows Dad a kiss, but he misses it.

His eyes are glued to his smart watch.

"Whoa, I just got another five-star rating on my recipe," he says, delighted, still staring at his wrist.

"Ah-hum." I clear my throat.

Dad jolts. "Oh. Yes! KyRose has something to tell us! Go on, mi amor."

Finally, I tell them everything.

"A team sport! I'm so proud of you," Mom says. "But *soccer*?"

She rolls her eyes at Dad who quickly cheers, "Fantastico! We just had no idea. Since when do you like soccer?"

"Well, it's a new thing," I say, tugging at my hair. "And, I have to do well!" I shoot up off my chair. "Can you please practice with me, Dad? Please!"

"Right now? Oh, mi amor. I can't." Dad splays his arms wide. "I've got to finish all this, then make my rounds at the Gut Love Juice shops." Dad now has seven of them around the city, including one a few blocks from MakerX20 and across the street from Jack's high school.

I don't bother asking Mom to kick the ball around with me. Clearly, she's way too exhausted. Only when I hear Alfred welcoming Jack home do my spirits lift. Surely, my big brother can give up skateboarding for an hour or two to help me out. Plus, he used to play soccer in middle school. Jack sidles into the kitchen. His crewcut hair is a dark shade of brown, except for the wavy bangs bleached orange-blond that hang over his brows. Jack wears a sleek, feather-light windbreaker custom made for him by RetroVibe. That's the streetwear label that now sponsors him since his last three videos went viral. Okay, my brother is famous. Or, at least popular enough to make Georgia giddy. Silver reflectors on his sleeve call out his handle: @rana_sk8r. The word *rana* means "frog" in Spanish. Abuela gave him the name when she first saw him do aerials. She said he was like the tree frogs leaping through the Amazon.

"Hiya," Jack says. "I am sooooo hungry."

I fold my hands on my lap and wait. Jack, like most teenagers, gets super irritable when he's hungry. He sniffs at the ice plants and crinkles his nose, then spins around toward the fridge. He taps "View" on the fridge screen, but before he can see what's inside, an ad starts to play.

A man's voice jingles in a sing-song beat, "The all new Think-It, from MetaTech, will keep you smart as a whip. With Think-It, you no longer have to talk or tap. Your thoughts instantly link to *all* your devices. They even link directly to the brains of other users. Simple wires, safe implants. Couldn't be easier."

"Or scarier!" Dad says, aghast eyes bulging. "Imagine a hacker seizing control? Turning us all into zombies."

"Dad, you watch too much sci-fi!" Jack scoffs and pulls open the fridge. He pops something crunchy into his mouth. As he keeps rummaging, Mom tells him about my news. Jack mumbles something back like congrats.

"So! You'll help me practice?" I ask. "Can you do it right now?"

Jack swivels round, stuffing a leftover burrito into his mouth. As he chews, he makes a fist and holds it up to his head, then grinds as though he were drilling into his skull.

I stare at him dumbfounded.

He swallows. "Guess Think-It ain't working yet!" He chuckles and adds, "Sorry, li'l sis." I it hate when he calls me that, and I can smell what's coming next. "I gotta go to Em's," he says. That's Jack's nickname for Emily, his spunky, brunette girlfriend. They've been an item since the end of ninth grade. Now in tenth, they're pretty much inseparable. Emily skates, too, but her real talent is camera and editing. She makes all of Jack's videos, including three that went viral. No wonder he can't leave her side.

"You going there to do homework or make movies?" Mom asks with a frown.

"Homework first, of course." Jack shoots her a grin that wins Mom over every time.

"Be home by nine o'clock. It's a school night," she

reminds him as her phone rings. Mom slides on her scopes to answer the call, which, of course, means she'll be on for a while.

Dad then ushers us all out of the kitchen. "Ahora mismo! I've got to finish this recipe." He commands the cameras back on. The juicer roars and I drag myself out into the living room. I throw myself onto the sofa. I guess I won't be able to practice after all. A moment later, the front door swings open. Puddles runs in, all white and fluffy, newly groomed, shaking his butt. He jumps into my arms. I give him the biggest hug ever. He smells like bubble gum.

"I'm so glad you're home." I say.

"Me too." He licks my face.

"Wanna play ball?" I ask.

"Definitely!" He jumps up. "But first, tell me…do I look handsome?" He twirls around.

"Yes, you do!" I give him a kiss. "And, guess what? You're not the only one looking good." I shimmy my shoulders like Georgia. As Puddles and I walk outside with a soccer ball, I tell him all about how I'm going to be popular. "Now, catch!"

Four

The Eagles

On the morning of our first game, I wake up excited. This is it! My chance to impress Georgia. We have to win. Of course, Georgia reminded everyone of this yesterday during practice. I have the skinned knees to prove it, slipping and sliding to block every ball.

Mom's voice booms through the sunflower speaker on my bedside table. "You up?"

"Yep!" I bounce out of bed and tap my shades. The sun streams in, and the turquoise beads on the kachina doll on my dresser glimmer in the rays of light. I look at the doll's painted eyes for courage. Maybe its spirit will lead me, the way it led the wounded puma through the forest to find the shapumvilla tree. Chewing on its leaves stopped the bleeding of the puma's paw. A story

Abuela told me.

Alongside the doll sits a stack of books. My favorite one is by Jane Goodall. She got to live with chimpanzees in Africa. How amazing! She was also the first person to discover that chimps make tools, just like humans. Next to her book is one that Dad gave me called *Silent Spring*. He even gave Cora a copy. It was written by Rachel Carson. She was a marine biologist with a strong voice who told the world how pesticides that were sprayed to kill mosquitoes actually killed other bugs too, like spiders and crickets. Birds like the robins ate the dead bugs and drank water contaminated by the poison. And then the birds, they died too! I covered my ears when Dad read that part aloud.

"I know it's tough to hear, mi amor," he told me. "But if we shut our minds off to what's happening around us, how will we ever see the problems of the world? And solve them?"

I guess he has a point. Rachel Carson spoke to the United States Congress to get laws changed about how pesticides were used.

Mom reminds me to hurry. I change into my soccer uniform. My jersey is lime green. Everyone else on the team will be wearing jerseys that are yellow and black, but Coach Hartley said because I'm goalie, I have to stand out. She also said we had to wear our uniforms to school on game days. There's a pep rally today. Before heading downstairs, I drop my duffle bag. Inside are my new gloves and cleats. Jack wanted me to get the neon ones. No way!. It's bad enough I have to wear this flashy jersey all day long.

I run up to the roof. Next to Dad's edible garden and compost are Abuela's rose bushes. I cut a flower for each of my teammates to hand out at the pep rally. I know red is Georgia's favorite color, so I cut her the "cherriest" one of all with the biggest petals. As I snip the last stem, I hear *Squawk! Squawk!*

Two bald eagles glide toward me with their wings spanning six feet.

"Gabriella? Merlin? Is that you?" I call out, shocked and delighted.

"Yes, it's us!" Gabriella says, landing on the railing beside me. Her head is covered with white feathers and her body with brown, and she stands three feet high. Merlin sets down beside her. She stands a few inches taller than him, like most female bald eagles she's larger than her mate. "See, I told you we'd find her!" Gabriella jabs him gently with her yellow beak.

"Yeah, yeah. After circling the shore for an hour, you finally figured it out!" Merlin grunts.

"Hey, you two. Stop bickering and tell me what brings you to the mainland?"

"We came to visit you, dear," Gabriella says.

"And to hunt," Merlin adds in a deep, determined

voice.

"I thought there was plenty of food on the island?" I ask. "With the great migration and all, weren't there lots of fish?"

"There were," Merlin says. "But not anymore."

"We used to fish with the dolphins," Gabriella adds. "But the pod must be off somewhere looking for food. So we thought we'd try our luck around here."

I reach for Dad's bin of seeds and offer them a handful.

"You first," Gabriella says, tipping her head toward Merlin.

"No. No. Go ahead, sweetheart," he insists.

As she bends her neck to eat, the nanobot tattoo peeks from beneath her feathers. It's still there so Troy can locate her.

"We sure have missed you, dear," Gabriella says, swallowing her last bite.

"Me too," I say, but just then Mom calls me from inside the house. "Sorry. I have to go!" I grab the roses. "Ouch!" I poke my finger on a thorn. "Come back. I'll be home after my game."

"Game?" Merlin cocks his head, but I'm already halfway down the stairs.

ಆ

That afternoon, twenty minutes before the game starts, I realize I don't have my cleats or my gloves! Shoot! I forgot my duffle bag, at home by the stairs. I call Mom. When the car rolls up to the curb, she holds my bag out the window.

"You need to keep track of your stuff," she says, annoyed, her eyebrows pinched together.

"I know. I know. I'm sorry," I say.

"I'm installing the update on Amigo, that digital assistant app I got you that runs on A.I. It'll keep you organized."

"No." Not that stupid thing. "I don't like artificial intelligence. C'mon, Mom! Remember how that dumb thing messed up my order and sent us twenty pairs of socks, instead of just the two I needed?"

"The new version is smarter," Mom says.

"Fine, whatever." I look at her. "Are you coming?" I expect her to be getting out of the car. "You're gonna watch me play, right?"

"Oh honey, I can't. I have my call with Mr. Sphinx." With her scopes on, she taps the time.

"What about Dad? Is he coming?"

"No. He's stuck at that vegan cheese conference. I'll call a car to pick you up after the game. You better go now before you're late again, like you were this morning."

"That wasn't my fault," I say. "I was on the roof and my friends dropped by for a visit."

Mom tilts her chin, looking grim. "What kind of

friends are those?" she asks.

I tell her.

"Oh, honey!" She reaches briskly out the window and squeezes my hand. "Imaginary friends? Fantasizing you can talk to animals? Abuela is gone. It's time for you to grow up and live in the real world."

I yank my hand away from her. Mom never believed. She thought it was cute when I was little, but she always thought I was playing pretend. Abuela told me that Mom just needed more time. She'd whisper in my ear, "One day, your mom will understand everything."

Well, I'm done waiting for that day to come.

Running under the bridgeway, my duffle bag slung over my shoulder, I roll onto the field. It looks bigger than at practice, and the bleachers are nearly full. Parents sit down below, and kids fill the rows higher up. There's Cora, head down, a curtain of hair covering her face. She bangs away on a tablet, likely coding another of her enchanted objects. Maybe a robot gumball machine? It'll be a hit. Especially if we give them out for free at school. Cora looks up, smiles. I wave back, glad she's here, at least I have one fan that'll be cheering for me. Further up are Dante and Dillon. Rex sits beside them, and all three wear their headsets playing *Smash Spectator*. Developed by a couple of whiz kids from

Finland, the game's been trending on FriendZ all month. It lets players maneuver virtually alongside real athletes at live sporting events. That's me! A real athlete. Kind of. I run over to the Jaguar's canopy. The bench is empty, and backpacks are strewn all around. Coach Hartley is standing by the sidelines shouting orders. Dang! I missed the kickoff. Maybe I should leave before anyone sees me? I mean, if I don't even try, that's not really *failing*. Is it?

Too late. The ref calls time out, and girls in uniforms jog off the field.

"Hey, you made it!" Rebecca says. She seems genuinely happy to see me.

"Ah, yeah," I reply and put on my cleats. They're still tight and stiff around my heels where I have blisters from breaking them in. Meanwhile, I keep a watchful eye on Georgia. She's fuming, but luckily not at me for being late. Her face is red hot as she stares down the sideline at the Victorians.

"Number nine. That's their star player," Coach says. "We need to cover her."

"That's Marta," Georgia blurts. "I got her!" She grits her teeth and stares back at Marta, the tallest girl on the Victorians' team. She's even more muscular than Georgia.

I remember what Cora said. Marta's the girl Georgia hates. The one from club soccer who bullied Georgia online.

"And number four, the redhead," Coach says. "She's short, but don't let that fool you. She's fast."

"Her name is Tommy," Georgia adds with grunt.

"I'll cover her," Avery says quickly and nods to Georgia. "Now that I don't have to fill in for you-know-who as goalie." Avery scoffs, looking at me. "Did you save a rat from the gutter or something? Is that why you're late?"

Everyone laughs. I turn away embarrassed, my blisters burning.

The ref blows the whistle.

"What you waiting for?" Coach asks me as I stand frozen. "Grab your gloves and get on out there. You got a goal to protect!"

At half-time, the score is still 0-0. The Victorians had two strikes on goal, both from Marta. Georgia knocked the first one out of bounds. Her mom cheered from the stands, waving her rhinestone-studded cap and yelling, "Way to go! Geor-jahhh!" The second kick, I blocked. My teammates cheered. It felt so great, like I was really part of the team, instead of stuck in the goalie box all alone. Now, as I take a sip of Dad's blueberry-aloe juice, Georgia walks over.

"Nice catch back there," she says. Her words hit me with more power and energy than any juice Dad could ever concoct. Georgia pats me on the back. Yep, I'm a part of the team!

As we start back up, a raindrop lands on my forehead. Georgia and Avery dribble the ball zig-zag across the field. Tommy steals it away. Georgia runs after her. But, then Marta trips Georgia.

"Foul!" Coach yells, but the ref ignores it.

Georgia's face turns beet red. She runs after Tommy. Elbows out, clamoring for the ball, Georgia retrieves it and scores. Woohoo! Our team and fans cheer. Even the *Smash Spectator* gamers stomp their feet. Georgia's mom applauds proudly. With her head held high, Georgia waves back at her. She then prances by Marta who leans over and says something. I can't hear what it is, but Georgia spits on the ground, angered by her words. During the next play, I lose sight of the ball. Behind a sea of legs and cleats, it pops back out, suddenly sailing past me and into our net. Oh no! The score is now tied, 1-1. Georgia clenches her fist and punches the palm of her other hand. Her fury ripples, smacking me in the chest. I catch my breath. With two minutes left on the clock, I pat my gloves. I've got this, I tell myself. Meanwhile, charcoal clouds move across the sky. The air cools and goosebumps spread over my shoulders. Marta has the ball. And, she is heading right towards me.

From the corner of my eye, I see a flash. *Wings*.

"Don't just stand there. Go get it," Merlin calls as he

and Gabriella swoop down and land on the crossbar above my head.

"What are you doing here?" I ask keeping one eye on Marta.

"We had to see your game, dear," Gabriella says. "We want to know all about it. If it's important to you, it's important to us."

My insides warm. I'm touched. Then I see Cora and some of the kids and parents in the stands pointing at the eagles. Even the gamers lift their arms like they're flying.

"Why are you just standing here?" Merlin asks. "Go get the ball." He tips his beak at Marta who now crosses mid-field.

"I can't. It's against the rules."

"What rules?"

"I'll tell you later."

"Well, it must be a hunting game," Merlin jabbers on. "To teach you how to hunt together, right?"

"Like us with dolphins, dear," Gabriella adds. "To capture dinner and chase away your prey. Isn't that right?"

"Not really. No. Maybe. I guess. Kind of." I shake my head. "I…I can't think. Not now!" I squint to focus on Marta and the ball. She passes it to Tommy. They dribble it back and forth, the wind on their backs. The clock ticks. With twenty-three seconds left in the game,

Georgia slides and knocks the ball away. Looks like the game will end in a tie.

Gabriella asks me if I'm having fun.

"Sure, she's having fun," Merlin answers for me and hops on my shoulder. I rub my cheek against his wings.

"I'm glad you came to watch me," I say. "You can meet my teammates." But then from the corner of my eye I see Marta running with the ball again. *Smack*! She kicks.

I lunge sideways. Merlin digs his claws into my shoulder then flies off as my gloves graze the ball. I fall to the ground. The Victorians cheer. The final buzzer rings. I can't bear to look back, but I do. The ball is in the goal.

Georgia stomps over, spewing like a volcano. "You freak! What's wrong with you? This is soccer, not some stupid petting zoo. I thought I could count on you. Obviously *not*!" She turns and marches off, covering her ears as the Victorians cheer on. Avery, Tabeen, and Rebecca stare wide-eyed at me, nodding their heads in disappointment. Then quickly, they turn and trail after Georgia.

I'm still lying on the ground.

Merlin and Gabriella hop down beside me. "Oh, dear," Gabriella says. "I'm sorry. I guess you lost your game."

"Shut up! Go away! It's all your fault!" I yell at the

eagles.

She and Merlin share a look of pain, then take off. A bolt of lightning streaks across the sky. A clap of thunder follows, unleashing a sheet of rain. The water mixes with the tears streaming down my face. Numb, I lie there, doomed. A freak. Where am I going to hide?

Five

Escape

In the car ride home alone, drenching wet, I come up with six ideas on how I can survive this mess that I got myself into.

1. I can run away and join the circus where all freaks are welcome; or

2. I'll show up tomorrow at MakerX20 in disguise, wearing tinted glasses and a hat. Surely, there's got to be a trench coat somewhere in our house, leftover from a Halloween costume, that I can wear. I'll speak in Spanish the whole day, pretending I just moved here from Nicaragua; or

3. I'll turn back time and replay the game. I won't talk to Gabriella or Merlin at all. Ignore them the whole time. (Too bad Cora hasn't invented a time machine

yet.); or

4. I'll beg forgiveness. No animals! No distractions. I'll convince Georgia that I *don't* speak to animals. Never did, never will! (Mom will like that too.) Then, I'll play damn good soccer. But Georgia doesn't forgive easily. There's Marta, and also poor Miriam, who's still on Georgia's hit list. Miriam tripped in the cafeteria on the first day of school. Her banana cream pie flung up into the air and landed plop onto Georgia's lap. Not good!; next idea

5. I'll tell Mom I'm sick. A simple cold will turn into a highly contagious strain of the flu. I'll have to be quarantined and stay home for the rest of the year. Of course, Mom will never go for this. She's way too busy to homeschool me. Alfred could be my teacher?; or

6. Last big light bulb in my head is…I'll transfer schools. There have got to be, at least, fifty other middle schools in the city. Should be easy.

Puddles greets me at the door wagging his tail. "How did it go?" he asks.

"Terrible!"

"Oh. Why?"

"Shh." I motion for him to keep quiet, as I hear Alfred's footsteps and listen for Mom's. Quietly, I pry off my sopping wet cleats and head upstairs. I step over Molly, our iMop. My socks slip on the polished treads. I grab the banister with a *thump*.

Mom calls from downstairs, "How did it go? Did you win?"

I freeze, instantly nauseous.

She's now at the bottom of the stairs looking up at me. "So?"

"Uhhh," I scramble.

A clap of thunder shakes the house. Puddles shivers by Mom's feet. I shiver, too, but for a different reason. I want Mom to be proud of me. I can't tell her the truth—that I was talking to the eagles, and that's why we lost the game. Thunder cracks again.

"Wow. I can't believe you were even able to play in this torrential storm." Mom says.

"That's it!" I blurt. "We...we couldn't finish. They stopped the game because of the rain." It just rolls out from my mouth...a lie, and it burns a hole in my chest.

"Well, go ahead and take a warm bath," Mom says, and walks back towards the living room.

Phew! Off the hook...for now anyway.

A trail of lavender follows me from the bathroom. Mom always keeps it stocked with lavender bath salts and soaps. As I step into my bedroom, the overhead lights pop on, way too bright. I reach to dim them when I hear, "Hel-lo Ky-Rose." The voice is stiff and robotic.

"Amigo?" I ask, shaking my head.

"Yes, I am back online," it says out of my sunflower speaker. Mom hasn't wasted any time. "I am fully functional, ready to learn and predict all your needs," it says.

"Really? Can you turn back time?"

"The time is 4:57 p.m."

"Great! That's all you've got?" Here I am, alone and rejected, on the precipice, falling down a cavern so deep and so narrow, no glitchy artificial intelligence (okay, call it A.I.) is gonna save me from Georgia's revenge. I'm never going to be popular now. I plop myself onto my bed, and slip my feet under my furry panda print blanket.

"Well, how about more socks then?" I ask, half joking.

"What color?"

"Forget it."

"Would you like to set up my voice?" it asks. "I have 783 options."

"Fine."

"I could be a boy," it says with a tad deeper tone. "Or your mom." The voice rises.

"Definitely not."

"How about a grandmother," it says in a doting, loving way. It doesn't have Abuela's *R*s rolling on the tip of the tongue. Still, it just makes me sad.

"Next," I say.

"How about a mouse," it says, all squeaky.

"No animals!" I shout.

"A New Yorker, an Irishman, an Italian," it goes on in different accents. Then finally, it suggests, "I could be your brother," with a perfect rendition of Jack. Creepy!

"No way!"

It rambles on. But then, I hear one. "Go back," I say.

"Big sister."

"That's it!"

It has a bright, warm tone with a tinge of an Australian accent, just like my favorite popstar Chandelle Waterhouse who I listen to on Stream-o-Rama. Chandelle has thirty million hearts and her song "The Grass is Always Greener" is my all-time favorite!

"How old would you like your big sister to be?"

"Sixteen," I say—same as Chandelle.

"All set. Now, give me a name. Anything you like."

Hmm? I close my eyes and breathe in. I see my five-year-old self sitting on a paisley green blanket beneath the oak tree in Abuela's old garden where she lived, before she moved in with us. I'm having a tea party with butterflies and beetles and my doll that I called Sarafina. I say her name aloud.

"I like that name. Now, hold on a sec," the A.I. says, already picking up the lingo. Then she goes silent. As I wait, my bracelet flashes. It's a video that Georgia posted on FriendZ, sent just to our soccer team. My finger trembles. I tap play and throw the video up onto the ceiling over my bed. Georgia is still wearing her soccer jersey. Though, it's completely dry and her lips shimmer with a fresh coat of lip gloss.

"I'm about to un-friend *someone*. And boot 'em from the team!" She leans into the camera. Of course, I know it's *me*. I play the video over and over just to torture myself. Then, I bury my face into my pillow.

Sarafina returns. "Alright, I am now fully integrated and have access to your smart devices and bio-scanners," she says, then adds, "Your heart rate is up. Are you okay?"

I don't answer.

"I'm here to learn all your needs," Sarafina says.

"Then find me a new school."

"Sure thing."

I sit up. "You can do that?"

"Sure, I'll scan databases across the school district, and see what I can find."

I smile and fall back on my pillow. Exhausted, my eyes grow heavy. As I drift off, I think of Cora. She never did run down onto the field when Georgia was yelling at me. Oh yeah, too much drama for Cora to stick her nose in. I guess I've got to fix things on my own now.

Six
Must Fit In

"Rise and shine," Sarafina says through the flowerpot speaker, straight into my head. Usually, it's Mom that wakes me up.

I pry open an eyelid. "What time is it?"

"7:01 a.m. and twenty-two seconds." Sarafina rolls my shades up.

"Stop. I'm not going to school! Roll my shades back down." I pull the covers over my head. Then it dawns on me. "Well, unless, you found me a new school?" I sit up.

"I reviewed every middle school this side of the city. Sorry, no openings."

"Argh! Sarafina! You suck!"

"I detect anger and frustration."

"You got that right!" I bite my nails. What am I

going to do? The smell of coffee trails into my room. That's it.

"Sarafina, fling Mom. Tell her I don't feel well."

"Done."

Mom fires back a reply. *What's wrong? Come on down for breakfast.*

"No! Tell her I'm *really* sick…but wait." She'll be mad. I'll mess up her day. Mom's got to get to her job site. But Alfred's here. He can watch me. "Send," I say.

Mom replies instantly. *I checked with Sarafina (nice name btw). Your heart rate is a bit high, but temperature and other biorhythms are all normal. You're going to school.*

"Thanks a lot, Sarafina!" I grab my digi-bracelet, flick over to the Amigo app, and tap disconnect.

On the car ride to school, I try once more.

"Mom, I don't feel well!"

"We already talked about this," she says without giving me even a glance. Mom's too busy tapping, confirming meetings, doing whatever her boss says. So much for the *quality family time* she said we'd have in the car. That was part of her pitch when she signed us up for the ShareCar club. The cars drive themselves, so we can look into each other's eyes. We're supposed to be *connecting*. But look at Jack beside me in his own world too. Wearing scopes, he's making plans with friends for after school. Jack makes being popular look so easy. I want to strangle him.

I stare out the window. Yesterday's storm has blown over. The sky is blue with a few brushstrokes of wispy clouds. It takes me a few seconds to notice that the clouds are actually moving. Abuela always said the earth is alive, ever-changing. Thankfully, there's no sight of Gabriella or Merlin, though a part of me feels really bad for chasing them away. I check my digi-bracelet for like the twentieth time. Georgia still hasn't *officially* un-friended me. Maybe, if I'm lucky, that storm has blown over too?

The car pulls up in front of MakerX20. "Okay, honey," Mom says. "If you do get sick, go to the infirmary. They'll check your vitals and call me."

No use stalling, I step out onto the curb. The car pulls away and here I am, alone…with 300 kids piling onto the lawn. They funnel toward the main entrance, peeling off their electronics—earbuds, headsets, personal scopes, smart-wear, and other bionics. Only school-issued devices are allowed inside. No outside tech, unless it's a medical necessity, like an insulin reader for diabetics. I see Tabeen peel off a baggy sweater right after her mom pulls away in her car. I then look for Cora, but don't see her anywhere. I don't see Georgia either. *Phew*!

Miriam hustles past me, her shirt untucked and her

hair all frizzy. Our eyes meet. She doesn't seem to hate me. Then again, she's not on the soccer team. I bend down, pretending to tie my laces, and wait for the other kids to go inside. By the jacaranda tree, a brown shadow zips across my path.

"Skinner! I almost stepped on you," I scold him, then look around to be sure no one's watching. The squirrel somersaults and rolls backwards. I can't help but giggle. He's my sunshine.

"You look pretty today," Skinner says with a shake of his spiny, brown tail.

"Are you flirting with me?" I ask, charmed by his affection. I reach into my pocket. Skinner sits on his hind legs and waits. I break the biscuit in half like always, and offer him a piece. He turns it round and round, chomping on it like corn-on-the-cob. When it's gone, Skinner tilts his head, twitching his pointy ears. I hand him the other half of the biscuit.

The bell rings. "I've gotta go," I say, feeling nauseous.

"See you after school," he calls, and dashes up the tree.

I drag myself up the stairs and through the double doors. They slam behind me with an ominous thump that echoes through the halls.

I make it past second period, and then in the hall, standing by my locker, I hear, "Hey, KeeRose. Hold up!"

With my hand quivering, I wave my locker shut. Georgia steps up, towering over me like the Statue of Liberty. But there's no freedom—she holds all the power. I remember the joy I felt yesterday with my teammates cheering me on. That was *before* we lost. Before Gabriella and Merlin showed up. I need a second chance. I'm not kicked off the team—not yet anyway.

I force a smile. "Hey there." My voice cracks. I clear my throat and use the extra second to scan her outfit: Bucci high-tops, tight jeans, and a red tank top. My eyes land on her backpack. "I, uh, uh, love your bag," I say, hoping a compliment will mend my mistake.

"Thanks! One of my mom's designs," she says with a shimmy, and I think it might be working. I follow the red rhinestones on her bag that form a dragon with a curved tail and fanged face. "Red is the color of power. My trademark," she says, but I already know that. Now it's her turn. She stands taller than ever and stares me up and down. I wish I hadn't worn these stained sneakers. Georgia then unexpectedly leans over and asks, "You don't *really* believe you can talk to animals, do you?" Her eyes narrow.

"I, uh, I like animals," I say, trying be at ease and *normal*. But my shoulders stiffen.

"Yeah, who doesn't, I guess. But you think you know what they're saying…for real?" The hall is empty. We're alone. She tips her head. There's something about the way she looks at me. After all, she has a secret too—ousted off that club team. I look deep into her eyes. Maybe, I can trust her?

"Hey, G," Avery calls from down the hall.

The next second, the Primas are crowding around us. "What's going on?" Avery asks with a suspicious sneer, her eyebrows zigzagging.

"Well, KeeRose here was just about to tell us if she's Snow White." Georgia chuckles, and I sigh.

"Oh, I like that princess," Tabeen says. "She has cute outfits."

Avery jabs her with her elbow. "Pathetic," she says, and rolls her eyes.

The girls scoot closer in a half-moon around me. The air turns hot. I feel sweat gushing in my armpits.

"Yeah, tell us," Avery says. "What did those eagles say to you yesterday?"

"'Come fly with me,'" Rebecca sings. It's a line from a cover song Chandelle just released. Rebecca's voice is just as melodic and beautiful.

But not to Georgia. "Save it for the shower!" she snickers.

Rebecca frowns.

I try and slip away.

"Hey, where are you going? Answer the question!" Georgia says, backing me into the lockers.

I feel dizzy. "No. What? I don't talk to animals! Are you kidding?" I exclaim. Dread seeps into my veins. I force a laugh. "Those birds, they're insane." I whirl my finger around next to my ear. Tabeen and Rebecca giggle. I go on. "Yesterday was a fluke. It would never happen again. Not in a million years." I look straight at Georgia to be clear she has my solemn promise. Then I change the subject. "Georgia you played a-maz-ing in the game."

She shimmies her shoulders and applies a coat of lip gloss.

I go on selling my soul. "And next time, we're gonna beat those Victorians," I say.

"You betcha!" Georgia flips her hand up. We seal the deal with a high-five. Yes! I'm back in. Phew!

At lunch, Cora and I sit at our usual table by the back wall. Above us is this quote:

"A person who never made a mistake
never tried anything new." —Albert Einstein

I tell Cora about the fatal end of yesterday's game. She tells me she left a few minutes early to avoid the rain. So, I guess I can't blame her for abandoning me.

"But the bald eagles were amazing," Cora says. "What did they say?"

"Nothing!"

"Oh, come on!"

"No really. I don't talk to animals anymore. And you better not tell anyone I ever did. Okay?" I hunch over the table, pleading.

"What are you talking about? I'd kill to have your gift. Why would you throw it away?"

"To go to Georgia's next party."

Cora shakes her head. "You're kidding, right? Who cares about her stupid party?" She takes a bite of her jackfruit enchilada.

"We do!" I say. "Now listen, I know what I'm doing." I sit up straight. "I just have to stay away from animals. That's all."

"Well, good luck with that." Cora laughs. "C'mon. They find you wherever you go. And what about Puddles? You gonna stop talking to him too?"

I hadn't thought of Puddles. My heart sinks. Home can be a safe zone. No one will see us. "Anyway, this is all just temporary," I say. "Once I'm popular, I can do whatever I want. You'll see."

"Sure, if you can remember who you are at the end. Popularity has a way of changing people. They start acting weird," Cora warns.

"Don't worry. That's not gonna happen to me." I take a bite of my burrito and feel the cashew cheese dripping slowly down my chin.

Seven

Adapt, or Die

After lunch, Cora disappears into the FabLab for her engineering class. I head next door to science. The smell of sulfur hits me like rotten eggs. High-top tables fill the room. Bunsen burners and test tubes line a counter. On the wall above are digital charts, like the periodic table of elements that has letters like O for oxygen, N for nitrogen, and Fe for iron. Another shows sound waves measured in frequency and hertz. A third chart maps out the electromagnetic spectrum—that's basically light. Narrow slivers highlight the tiny bits of the spectrum that humans can hear and see.

Windows in the back of the room stream sunlight onto the bio-domes we've been growing. Georgia and Avery are already sitting together. I inch my way closer and slip onto a stool beside Georgia.

Ms. A calls roll, tapping at the holographic screen that floats across her desk. "Dante, Dillon, Will…." She speaks in a British accent. It's fainter than Alfred's, yet still prim and proper. The teacher sits up straight in her chair, her skin is brownish-black like the ink of an octopus, and her body petite. Her hair is pulled back in a bun that makes her look older, at least in her late 20's. Ms. A always wears the traditional dress of India, a sari. It's a long skirt with a matching blouse that twists and flaps over her shoulder. On the first day of school, we so badly butchered her name (Ms. Argawal) that she reluctantly gave in, letting us shorten it.

I know the feeling. Georgia still mispronounces my name. I should correct her, but oh well. Now catching a whiff of her apricot conditioner, I use the sweetest voice I can muster. "Wow, your hair is so shiny."

"Thanks," Georgia says, tossing her head back. She and Avery then talk about her next party. My heart thrums. The conversation moves on to the latest FriendZ fads. I rack my brain to come up with makeup brands—anything to jump into the conversation—but most of the ads I get served are for panda slippers or some kind of camping gear like mosquito netting. Nothing Georgia would ever be interested in.

Ms. A sips from a cup of her cardamom-ginger tea, then tells us to fetch our bio-domes. "Today, you'll be taking final measurements as we wrap up this unit." For the past three weeks, we've been studying photosynthesis and the nitrogen cycle of plants.

Will is the first up. His stool screeches across the floor. Georgia shouts to Miriam to get theirs. Fate had it that they were partnered up. Poor Miriam. I stay put, saving my spot next to Georgia. Will brings over our model. It's a glass bowl filled with soil, fungi, blue-green algae, and a baby fern that's now much taller since we planted it from seed. Georgia doesn't seem to notice the newfound height of her fern as Miriam stumbles over with it. Instead, she sniffs around Miriam's bushy, brown hair.

"What the jive is that?" Georgia reels with a hand covering her nose.

"Oh!" Miriam bursts. "It's my lavender-oregano perfume. You like it? I made it myself." There's a naive twinkle in her eye as she grins. Plastic aligners and neon rubber bands fill her mouth. Unfortunately, food and gum are stuck inside. I cringe, wanting to run next door to the FabLab to print her another pair. But of course, it's too late.

"Gross! Miriam, shut your mouth. You're so useless," Georgia scoffs, and then glances my way. Lips tight, I brush my tongue over my teeth before smiling back.

Ms. A hands out a box of fingertip sensors. "Use

these along with your school scopes to measure the nitrogen levels and pH balance of your plants. Remember, the plants in your bio-domes are competing for nutrients, but also have to rely on each other. That's the delicate balance of a healthy ecosystem."

I put on my scopes. Through them, everything is magnified. Goosebumps run over my shoulders. This is how scientists must have felt 400 years ago when they first invented the microscope and were able to peek into a world they'd never seen before, or even knew existed. With a tingle in my throat, I watch as the moldy fungi in our bio-dome slurps up the nitrogen bits from a fallen leaf that lies crumpled on the soil, halfway decayed. It works just like inside Dad's compost. And, like a soccer ball, the nitrogen gets passed from one teammate to the next. The circle of life—it goes round and round.

"Nitrogen is vital to plant growth," Ms. A says.

"Like fertilizer," someone calls out.

"Yeah, that's right. But not too much or your plants will die," Ms. A adds stepping to the front of the room.

Next, I clip the sensor over my finger and touch the soil. This sensor measures the pH balance—the alkaline and acidity levels—of the soil.

"Whoa!" Will exclaims. The bar across our shared dashboard spikes red. "What?! That didn't happen when I touched it. That algae's got a crush on you! Hey, Ms. A," he shouts. "Check this out."

Georgia cranes her neck. I kick Will under the table. "Ouch!"

Ms. A walks over, and I kick him again. He frowns, but luckily gets the message. "Uhh, nothing. My mistake," Will grumbles. As Ms. A walks away, he rubs his shin. I mouth a silent thank you. Later, as we put away our project, he leans over and whispers, "I get it. We all have secrets."

But I don't wonder what Will's secret might be as I follow Georgia out into the hall. We have only a five-minute break. By the vending machine, Rebecca pauses to read a notice about chorus tryouts coming up.

Georgia then asks me, "What was going on with Will?"

"Oh nothing!" I point to the vending machine. Dangling behind the glass is Dad's flax-seed and goji-berry chips. I flick my digi-bracelet and buy two bags each for Georgia, Avery, Tabeen, and Rebecca. It costs more LunaCoins than I usually spend in a whole week on snacks, but I figure it's a good investment in my future. I bury the guilt of the bribe further, chalking it up as marketing for Gut Love Foods, like when Dad gives out free samples. Except this time, I'm paying for it.

When we return to class, Ms. A slides open the dividing wall that separates the science lab from the FabLab—the engineering class's fabrication laboratory. I wave to Cora. She smiles and waves back.

"What's up with science joining us?" someone yells from Cora's side of the room.

"It's called immersive learning, dummy," Avery shouts back. At MakerX20, teachers mix-in all kinds of subjects—math, science, language arts, and history—into the projects we work on. I like it because it makes school less boring and shows us how things are connected.

Mr. Bracket, the engineering teacher who runs the FabLab, skips to the front of the room, now combined into one big open space. Mr. Bracket stands a foot taller than Ms. A. He's African American, has tight curly hair, and a freckled face. He wears overalls, and tools dangle from loops around his pockets. With his sleeves rolled up, Mr. Bracket rubs his knuckles.

"So! For this next project, we're headed far, far away—all the way to Mars," he announces, eyes sparkling.

"For real?" Dillon shouts.

"No, stupid!" Dante knocks his twin in the head.

"Well, maybe when the colony's up and running." Mr. Bracket smiles, delighted. "And you're a bit older."

"You'll never be older than me," Dante brags to his

brother.

Dillon slumps in his chair. "Fifteen seconds—that's all you beat me by, bro," he scoffs under this breath. I get it. Sometimes being born second can suck. I walk in Jack's shadow all the time.

Ms. A goes on to explain how Mars—like Dante—isn't all that friendly to humans…or really any life we know of. The planet is extremely cold, minus eighty degrees Fahrenheit. Brrr! And deadly radiation is constantly streaming in from the sun because Mars doesn't have a magnetic field oozing from its poles like we do here on Earth to shield it. Mars also has huge dust storms and the atmosphere has only 1% oxygen—compare that to Earth where we have 21% oxygen.

"The astronauts on Mission Colonia land on Mars in just fifty-five days," Ms. A says. "They'll have to convert carbon dioxide to oxygen, make water, and grow their own food—all in an enclosed habitat, just like your bio-domes."

"And when they do go outside." Mr. Bracket throws open a window, ready to leap. "Wait! They first have to wear protective gear so the radiation doesn't eat them alive, and also so they can keep breathing and stay warm. And they need special gadgets to explore. Who knows what they'll find? Imagine yourself, an explorer on Mars!" He lifts a finger to the sky.

Are you kidding? I can barely survive Earth.

I pass Georgia a note. On it, in blinking bubble letters, I've scribbled "Victorians suck!" That gets her attention. Georgia shoots me a thumbs up. Then I see Cora watching us.

Mr. Bracket tells us about the GoMars competition. It's for students around the globe, and we'll be participating. The mission: use design thinking to brainstorm and build prototypes for tools and gadgets that are Mars-proof.

Winners of the competition get to send their final designs to the astronauts, who'll actually try them for real, Mr. Brackets tells us as he rubs his knuckles again. Will kicks me under the table. He raises his eyebrow. He's doesn't actually think he can win, does he?

Mr. Brackets plays a recorded clip from Captain Marco, who's on the spaceship zooming through space.

"Hello, kids," Captain Marco says, dressed in black spandex jumpsuit. "Glad you're taking on this mission. Can't wait to see your inventions. Enjoy the ride!"

The clip ends, and Ms. A announces our homework over the weekend—to watch videos and read up on Mars stuff and the kind of gear astronauts will need. "And Monday," she says, "we'll be going on a field trip to do more research. Plants and animals here on Earth adapt to all kinds of severe conditions. Rain, drought, freezing cold, desert heat. Their genes mutate, and they pass on favorable traits to their babies. Charles Darwin called it natural selection."

"Survival of the fittest!" Dante jumps up, flexing his bicep.

"An ecosystem is also about balance. Not just beating each other out," Ms. A snaps.

"Yeah, don't get greedy, Dante!" Rex calls out.

"He can't help it," Dillon mutters.

Ms. A clears her throat and goes on, "Plants and animals when they adapt create superpowers. Like thorns on a porcupine who rolls into a ball to protect itself when a bear comes stalking. Or, the way a skunk sprays a stinky…."

"Phew! Rex! I can smell that superpower from here," Dante shouts, fanning his hand wildly. The room erupts in laughter. Rex rocks back in his chair trying to act chill. He pats his spiky coif, purple today.

"Alright, settle down!" Ms. A orders, thumping her hands as if she were pounding on a piano.

When the room quiets, Mr. Bracket tells us how engineers love nature. He picks up a cactus plant from his desk and pretends to kiss it. Too close. Ouch! We all laugh. "But seriously," he says, "we copy nature all the time…to solve problems. Take your gym shorts, for example. They never get dirty. Why?" Hands go up, but no one gets the answer. He goes on, "It's because the fabric is made like a lotus plant. Tiny bumps on the surface of the plant—and in your case, the fabric of your shorts—keep water from soaking through. So instead, the water beads up and sucks up dirt and dust. When it rolls away, your clothes stay clean."

"To copy nature like that is called biomimicry," Ms. A says. "And that's how we want you to come up with ideas for your Mars projects."

"Hey, my dog has 300 million smell receptors in its nose," someone calls out.

"Yeah, but how's that gonna help you on Mars, idiot?" Dante reams.

"You can do more research on the field trip," Ms. A says. "We're going to the Animal Safe Haven. A friend of mine who I went to high school with runs the place."

Wait! That's got to be Troy, the biologist I met over summer. He said he ran a place called the Safe Haven. He even invited me to visit. But I totally forgot, I've been so antsy about school starting. Maybe, during the fieldtrip I can ask him about Gabriella and Merlin. And if he gives me Gabriella's GPS, I could track her. Then I'd never be caught off guard at a game again.

Cora raises her hand. "Are we gonna have partners?"

"Glad you asked," Ms. A says. "You'll be working in teams of three or four. Look for classmates that complement your skills."

"You mean we can pick our own partners?" Georgia asks.

"Yes," Ms. A says and when she looks away, Georgia sticks her tongue out at poor Miriam.

"Well, I know who I'm picking!" Georgia exclaims. Popping off her stool, she walks straight to Cora. I get up and follow her. "Coralina," Georgia says. "you will be my partner! Miriam was worthless, but I know you'll do an awesome job. You can code anything, right?!"

"Excuse me?" Cora leans back in her chair. I barely notice the shock across her face because all I can think of it how perfect this is going to be. Me, Georgia, and Cora—partners? We'll be best friends in no time, and throw a party all together. Or at least, for sure, Georgia will invite us to her next party. But then, Cora stands up, and I can't believe the words coming out of her mouth. "You think you can order me around like one of your minions?" The room goes quiet. Everyone turns and looks at us. "I'm not your slave, you know," Cora says. "I'll pick my own partner, thank you very much!"

Someone whistles from the back. Georgia's face turns red. She huffs and stomps off. I cringe as I roll my eyes. How could Cora ruin everything in a split second? Cora shrugs. Clearly, she doesn't want to be popular! I have to grab the side of the table to steady myself as I lose my balance. It feels like the earth just split open beneath my feet.

When I get home, Puddles follows me to my room. I toss my JellyGlobe backpack onto the bed. With no one spying on us, I tell him about my day. Of course, I leave out the part about swearing I would never speak to animals.

I then turn Sarafina back on and tell her I no longer need a new school. "Just get me my soccer schedule. I can never be late again!"

"No problem," she says. "I just hope you don't get mad and shut me off like you did this morning."

"What do you care? You're just a computer."

"I'm programmed to have feelings."

"You are?"

"Yes, and I felt, well, rejected. But now…you like me again and I feel happy." She giggles, but it sounds awkward and mechanical.

Sarafina admits, "I don't know what to do with all these emotions anyway. They're so foreign—and frankly, illogical?"

"What does that mean?" I ask.

"No logic. Emotions don't have rules like math. They spiral around with multiple outcomes," Sarafina says.

Puddles jumps on the bed. "Who are you talking to?" He sniffs the flowerpot speaker.

"Don't be jealous." I kiss his wet and cold nose.

Sarafina clears her throat, as though she had one. I introduce the two of them. Of course, Puddles doesn't understand everything she says. He has a limited human vocabulary. Jack says it's thirty words at most. And Sarafina can't understand dog. But through the cameras in the house and his smart collar, she confidently adds, "I'll keep an eye on Puddles. I'll make sure he gets scheduled walks and meals, and not too many treats."

Puddles barks.

"Just don't turn me off," Sarafina says.

"Okay. But you know I have to during school hours," I remind her.

"Yes, of course. You have to follow the rules."

My digi-bracelet rings. It's Cora. I sigh. Why did she have to make a fool of Georgia in front of the entire class? My bracelet keeps ringing, and my finger waffles back and forth over the buttons: accept or deny. With a heavy heart, I hit one. And I know I just broke a rule. A big one.

Eight

Balancing Act

On Monday morning, I board the bus for the field trip. Most of the seats are already taken. Georgia and Avery sit together a few rows down, toward the middle of the bus. Avery is turned, faithfully braiding Georgia's long, golden strands into pigtails. Cora waves at me from the back, an open seat beside her. But I can't move. Feet locked, I stand in the aisle at the front of the bus. Cora keeps waving and tips her head with a puzzled look.

Meanwhile, someone's brought a beach ball onboard, and kids take turns punching it up and down the aisle. The ball sails past me, a swirl of red, yellow, and white. It carries me back to memories of summer days when Cora and I used to play for hours at the beach. We'd dig for crabs. They'd tickle our fingers. Then we'd build sandcastles and take turns burying each other in the sand. We learned to bodysurf and dove under the waves to swim with schools of anchovy. Later, exhausted, we'd eat almond butter sandwiches beneath Abuela's burlap umbrella. Life was simple. No one judged us back then.

Inside the bus, the air conditioning is blasting. I zip up my bamboo sweatshirt, and look away from Cora. I slide into the first open seat. The kid sitting next to me has on a Chicago Bears hoodie. It's pulled up over his head so I can't see his face. Between his fingers, he wields a LibRik-Cube, twisting and turning the color-coded panels with lightning speed. Suddenly, the kid springs out from under his hoodie, his hair mussed like a young Albert Einstein. It's Will.

"Hey! I bet you're excited." He grins.

"What are you talking about?" I ask.

"You kidding?" He shoves the puzzle into his pocket. "There's gonna be a million animals where we're going." He elbows me. "Go on. Tell me how you do it?"

"Do what?"

"That voodoo communicado thing." He wriggles his fingers up in the air. "Heard you talk to squirrels and now eagles too."

"What?! Shut up!" I look around. Spies everywhere.

"It's okay. I already know the truth. Algae don't lie.

Whaddya got antennas up there?" He flicks my cap. The one from Camp Catalina. I wore it to help Troy remember who I was. But now, I tug it down hard so it covers my eyes. I fold my arms. Will nudges again. "Sorry. I shouldn't make fun of you. Honestly, I'm just curious." He seems sincere. "Tell me. I promise to protect you."

"Protect me?"

Just then, the beach ball hits him in the head. We look back at the same time. There's Dante, three rows behind, snickering.

"You got enough to worry about, don't you think? And protect me from what, anyway?" I ask.

"You mean *whom*." Will shifts and points at Georgia.

"Stop!" I grab his arm. "Fine! I'll tell you." In a hushed voice, I share with him the way Abuela explained it to me. "There's a place called *The Zone* where time slows. Sometimes it feels like time stops altogether. When I fall into it…I can, well, hear what animals say. Not all of them, of course."

"And, they can hear you too? They actually understand what you're saying?"

"Yeah, but it's no big deal." Though we both know it is, and I have to make it go away. I have to blend in. Thank goodness Ms. A interrupts us.

"Good morning, everyone," she says as the bus

lurches forward. "Once we get to the Animal Safe Haven, remember to look for *superpowers* that will help our astronauts live on Mars."

"You're on a mission," Mr. Bracket chimes in. "Think Red Planet. Power. Electricity. Oxygen. What else do you need? What other *problems* do you have to *solve* in order to survive and explore Mars? You'll need to see far distances, into the dark, and through dust storms. What about moving heavy boulders? Flying over bumpy terrain? Digging underground in search of precious metals and frozen lakes? Who knows…your inventions might even be used here on Earth—like Teflon non-stick cooking pans and the cameras in our cell phones and drones. Both came out of the space programs back in the 1970s, and now we use 'em every day."

The bus swerves onto Marine Way. Hundreds of boats, parked in slips, lined up like soldiers, loom into view.

"One more thing," Ms. A adds. "Start thinking about who you want to partner up with."

Will taps my arm. "We should team up. With your voodoo, I bet we could win the GoMars competition and show Dante what an idiot he is, 'cause he could never win."

"Uhh, I'm gonna be partners with Georgia," I cough up, glancing quickly back at her as Avery ties her braids.

"You two already figured that out?"

"Well, no. But I don't care if I have to do all the work. It's going to be worth it when I go to her party."

"What party?"

"The one she's planning, silly."

"Oh, well, maybe I can still join your team?"

"No. I mean, maybe." I shrug. I don't want to hurt his feelings, but there's no way.

The bus rumbles on, and we pass by a construction site. Twice the size of our soccer field, right on the water. Bulldozers are busy knocking down an old apartment building. Guess Mom got her permits. On the chain-link fence that wraps around the dirt-covered lot is a huge sign that reads: *Oyster Village…coming soon*.

"Did you hear?" Will pipes up. "They're gonna take over."

"Take over what?"

"My dad works for the city. He told me Oyster Village is gonna take over the Safe Haven. At least, well, that's what they're trying to do."

"What?!" My head spins.

"Yeah, they want to snatch it up to build a gaming arena there." The bus turns into the parking lot of the Safe Haven. Mom wouldn't do that. She wouldn't push the animals out. I tug at my hair, twirling the strands.

"What's wrong?" Will asks.

I shrug and keep quiet. He doesn't need to know that my mom runs construction for the Oyster Village. Anyway, I bet it's her mean boss that's making her do it.

The bus comes to a halt. Three warehouses connect together to make up the Safe Haven. The parking lot is entirely empty except for a lone pickup truck. Troy stands beside the truck talking to the fisherman, Frankie, who leans with his foot up on the back fender. A decal on it blinks *#MaidenVoyageFishery*, but the bed of the truck isn't filled with fish. Instead, there's a mound of metal scraps, like you'd find at a junkyard or maybe in the garbage bins of a robot factory—Alfred's nightmare. In the pile of scraps are rusty gears, sockets, a dirty shaft, broken lights, and the blades of a dented propeller poking out from one end. The parts remind me of the Lego pieces Jack and I used to snap together to make our toy trains. That was before he ever had a girlfriend of course, and had plenty of time to play with me.

Troy taps his foot and moves his hands all animated as he talks. He's clearly excited about something. Under his white lab coat, he wears a camouflage shirt with a crisp bowtie and khaki shorts. His brassy-colored hair and goatee match his tortoise-framed scopes, the same ones he wore on the island. I wonder if he'll remember me.

Suddenly, I hope he doesn't! I hold my stomach as it

tumbles like cartwheels. What was I thinking? There's no way I can ask Troy about the eagles. Not with Georgia around!

Ms. A, waves at Frankie and Troy from her seat two rows up from us. Frankie looks down at his shredded, worn-out shoes. As the doors of the bus open, he gives Troy a quick fist bump, climbs into his truck, and drives off in a hurry, hauling his heavy load.

Troy greets Ms. A as she steps off the bus. His orange bowtie seems to highlight the honeysuckle flowers printed on her wrap blouse. I step off the bus behind her, then quickly turn away so Troy can't see my face, but I catch snippets of their conversation.

"Was that Frankie?" Ms. A asks.

"Yep," Troy answers.

"I haven't seen him since high school. Why didn't he stay and give me a proper hello?"

"I think he's embarrassed," Troy says.

"Embarrassed? Why? I love that guy."

"Oh, c'mon. You're pretty pushy and have high standards, you know that." Troy clears his throat.

"Pushy? I'm encouraging," Ms. A says. "Frankie had a brilliant future ahead of him. I can't believe he dropped out of college just to help his father out on that fishing boat."

"Not everyone has the same path to success," Troy says.

"But, Frankie's a genius," Ms. A says. "Remember in

high school, how when he was only a freshman and we were seniors, how he hacked into West Oil's computer system? Remember, he found out exactly when the CEO would be on the oil rig so we could boycott their offshore drilling at the perfect moment?"

"How can I forget?" Troy says. "The three of us on our paddle boards, holding up signs for Greenpeace, tweeting 'Save the Ocean.'"

"It was definitely an adventure." Ms. A giggles. I don't think I've ever heard her laugh before.

"So, you had fun letting your hair down?" Troy asks impishly. Kids hurtle past them.

"We'd better go inside," she says tucking a loose strand of her hair back into her bun.

The lobby smells of kitty litter and straw with a hint of moss. One of the walls is covered by a mural of a redwood forest. Tall trees and lush ferns sway ever so slightly. The mural then fades out, and another appears in its place. It's of a coral reef with fish of all colors.

"Hey, hold up." Cora grabs my shoulder. Uh-oh, here it comes. "Why didn't you sit with me on the bus?"

"Um. Sorry." My heart races. I scan around for Georgia. There she is next to the welcome desk. She snaps her fingers, calling me over.

Cora follows my gaze. "What? We're not friends anymore now that you're hanging out with *her*?"

"Of course we're friends. Maybe you and I just need

to take a break. I mean…just…until soccer season is over." I stumble over my words.

"Are you kidding? I told you. I'm not kissing up to her just to be popular!" Cora lashes out. "And you shouldn't either!"

"Suit yourself. But I gotta go." I push through the crowd.

Ms. A introduces Troy as Dr. Merryweather, a bio-ecologist.

"Hey kids. First off, call me Troy. No formality here." He winks at Ms. A, then goes on. "So, you're here to do research for Martian gear. Very cool!" He looks back at Ms. A and this time smiles at her. Then he tells us all about how they have over 300 species of birds, reptiles, mammals, and fish at the Safe Haven. Most are here because of habitat loss from wildfires and flooding due to global warming. Or, from bulldozers tearing up the land for new construction. Troy then asks, "Any questions?"

"Are any of the animals hurt?" someone asks.

"We've got an owl with a broken wing and you'll see others too." Troy peers around the room. I duck behind Georgia's braids and listen from there.

"Once they recuperate, we try to release the animals back into the wild. Ideally, into sanctuaries and habitats that are protected by the government."

"Hey, what's that over there?" Rex asks. He points at

two men wheeling a glass container topped with a screen.

"A sixteen-foot Burmese python," Troy says, "smuggled into the country by poachers." Kids bend over each to catch a glimpse of the brown-spotted snake coiled up inside. As the two men pass by Will, Dante shoves him. "Dare ya to put your hand in there! Willy, willy, will ya?" Dante taunts.

"Uh, maybe later," Will mutters, and shoves his hands into his pockets as everyone laughs. Everyone except Cora, that is.

Troy tells us we're free to roam. There are five chambers, each a different biome—grasslands, desert, rainforest, tundra, and ocean. "The ocean one is our largest, 'cause we're right here on the marina," Troy adds.

A hand shoots up. Rex again. "Can we use drones to video stuff?" He probably just wants to post on FriendZ.

"Sure, just keep a respectful distance," Troy says. "Animals can bite—or worse—if they're feeling attacked. I don't want anyone getting hurt."

I follow Georgia and Avery into the grasslands chamber.

"Hey look." I show them a three-banded armadillo. "Their front claws are super sharp. They use 'em to rip open termite mounds and tree bark," I say.

"How do you know that?" Avery snaps.

"Oh, I must've seen it on a nature show or something." My voice dips. "Anyway, it'd be great for digging on Mars, right?"

"Ew. Look! It's defective!" Georgia says, reeling back.

I crouch down beside the armadillo. Mesmerized, I watch its ears flicker and its olive-shaped eyes stare straight into mine. Georgia suddenly kicks the glass with her boot. The armadillo jumps, and I fall back—both of us startled. Then I see it. The tips of its claws are missing, snapped off.

"That's not sharp enough for our project," Avery says with a smirk. She and Georgia stomp off.

"Don't take it personally," I say. "They don't know better. You're special just the way you are." I blow the armadillo a kiss, then dash after the girls.

In the desert biome, a group of boys, including Will, huddle around Mr. Bracket as he points at a viper. "See the holes between its eyes? Those are pits," Mr. Backet explains. "They sense heat. Snakes use 'em to find warm-blooded animals in the night when they hunt."

"Any chance those pits can find cold stuff, too, like a frozen lake on Mars?" Will asks. He sees me coming and raises his eyebrows. Quickly, I check on Avery and Georgia. Both are busy sneaking peeks at their digi-bracelets—checking their FriendZ feeds, no doubt. I shake my head at Will. No go. Anyway, I wish he'd just find another partner.

When Georgia and Avery go to the bathroom, I wander into the rainforest biome to find a *superpower* to impress them. The air is hot and sticky. A family of green parrots hop along the branches of a mango tree. A sloth tightens its curl around the limb of a fig tree. Sloths sure love to sleep, snoring fifteen to eighteen hours a day. That's way too long for an astronaut who has to explore Mars. I walk deeper into the tropical smells…coconut, banana, sweet flowers—they seep into my nose. I remember stories Abuela would tell of how when she was a little girl, she'd follow the elders into the jungle in search of herbs and medicine. Flocks of toucans would show them the way. I wonder if Abuela is with the toucans now. Mom and Dad could be wrong. Maybe Abuela is coming back—when she's all better.

"Ca-caw!" Perched on a branch, a scarlet macaw screeches. Its body and head are a fire-engine red, and its wings rainbow, like the snow cones they sell at carnivals. "Ha-llo. My name is Mabel," she says in a gravelly voice. "What's your name?"

I first look around to be sure we're alone, then whisper my name to her.

"I'zz got a lee-tle itch? Vould you mind?" Mabel says, tipping her neck toward me.

I reach up on my tippy toes. Holding out my pinky, I scratch her neck. She coos and her feathers puff. On my finger, I feel her hollow bones vibrate like the strings of a violin.

"How did you end up here at the Safe Haven?" I ask.

Mabel tells me how she was stolen away—from brothers and sisters, aunts and uncles, and her parents—by poachers. They then smuggled her out of Costa Rica and into the United States, where she was sold in a pet store to a woman, whom she lived with for twenty years. When the woman died, Mabel was brought here.

"T'izz not a bad place. Oh, but *mi corazon*," she wraps a wing over her heart, "izz back in mi jungle." She closes her eyes softly.

"That's far away. I wish I could help you get back there," I say.

"Izz o-kay, just nice that you listen. You are different." Mabel fans her wings as though she were about to give me a hug, when a stampede of boys led by Rex come crashing through the ferns. Green parrots scatter to the ceiling.

"Hey, Snow White, is that your newest feathery friend?" Rex shouts. "Did she tell you her *superpower*? What is it?"

The boys laugh.

Panicked, I tell Mabel I have to go.

"Promise, you'llz come back?" Mabel asks.

But there's no time to answer. I run off. Behind me, I hear Rex say, "Hey, birdie, birdie."

Then, "Squawk!"

And a loud yelp, "Owww!"

I fly out of the rainforest and smack into Troy.

"Oh, you okay?" he says, and reaches out his arm to help me up. "KyRose? Is that you?"

"Uh. Hi, Troy."

"Oh my gosh, it is you. The girl who held that bald eagle…Gabriella, right?"

I nod and look around to see who might be listening. Troy strokes his goatee, pondering something. "Hey, I want to show you something," he says. "Come with me."

Georgia follows us.

Nine

Meeting Misty

Troy leads me through a door and down a hallway. At the end is a second door. The sign on it says *Ocean Biome & Lab*.

"Oops, forgot to unlock it," Troy says. A camera scans his face. The door clicks open, and Troy holds it as I walk in, followed by Georgia, Avery, and then Will and Cora.

"Wait for me. I want to see," Ms. A calls out with her heels tapping.

Inside the lab, it's cold and damp, and smells of salt. Along the left side of the room, blue lights glow over rows of glass aquariums and plastic tubs. Water gurgles through filters. Jellyfish, eels, shrimp, and all sorts of reef fish swim inside the tanks. The swirly patterns along their skin—bright orange, red, and green—are in high contrast under the blue lights. Troy calls it bioluminescence.

Further in the room, all along the front, are windows with a panoramic view of the marina. No wonder Mr. Sphinx wants to get his claws on this place. He could charge a fortune for rent. Though gaming arenas…they don't even really have windows. But Mom's hot-shot boss must know what he's doing.

Outside the lab, on the other side of the windows is a wide deck with a huge, round aquarium. Part of it jets beneath the windows and into the lab. So, it's part inside and part out. The aquarium is big, like the ones at Ocean World in San Diego. Abuela and I went there, but only once. It was so sad watching the dolphins and whales stuck in captivity, forced to do tricks just to please the audience.

I hear a splash and wonder if that rescued dolphin that I saw on my newsfeed is actually still here. I take a few steps toward the tank, but Ms. A points in another direction and asks Troy a question. So I follow the group toward the back of the lab instead, where a long, skinny desk is strewn with messy piles of paper and yellow Post-it notes. Just above the desk are eight rectangular monitors mounted on the wall. Red dots flash across the screens and emit beeping sounds. "What are those for?" Ms. A asks.

"That's our GPS tracking system," Troy says.

One of the lights has to be Gabriella. I scan the dots, but beneath are only numbers, no names. If I could just ask Troy. But not with Georgia here! She strolls by with her arm stretched wide, and slides it through the holographic prism that projects two-feet up high over a square table, just past the desk. The speckled beams of light break up and reform into what looks like a mountain range. Troy explains that the hologram is a map of the ocean floor around the Channel Islands. There are eight islands in total and Catalina is the closest to us here on the mainland.

Past the table with the hologram are three VR cockpits. Each has a saddle seat. A shielded helmet hangs from each of their handlebars. They look like motorcycles but without wheels. Instead, they sit on a gyroscope and can spin in any direction. I know, 'cause Jack's got one in his bedroom. He converts it to practice skate tricks, and we used to take turns playing the video game *River Rambler*.

"What are these for?" Cora asks, wide-eyed as she strolls over to the cockpits.

"Oh, those puppies," Troy says. "They're for driving our ROVs when they're not on autopilot."

"ROVs? You mean *remote operated vehicles*?" Will asks. "Like the mobile labs crawling all over Mars?" His face lights up and he looks over at me. I turn away.

"Yeah. Just like on Mars," Troy says, "but ours swim underwater. We've got twenty-five ROVs in our fleet, all swimming out there around the islands."

"What do they do?" Cora asks.

"Count fish, check the pH balance in the water—to see if the alkaline and acidic levels are healthy enough for fish and plankton to grow. The ROVs also measure how much plastic is floating out there."

"So you look at the whole ecosystem?" Ms. A asks.

"That's right," Troy says. "And, we share the data with scientists around the world through our A.I. network. Thing is, lately, something really weird is happening around the islands." Troy scratches his head. "It's a mystery. First, we had this great migration with record numbers of mackerel showing up all summer. The mackerel attracted the dolphins, sharks, whales, and lots of other big fish like yellowfin tuna. Feeding frenzy. Mackerel for everyone! Lured fisherman here too. I was trying to figure out why so many mackerel would just show up like that. And then, poof!"

"The fish are gone!" I blurt. Everyone looks at me.

"How did you know that?" Troy asks.

Of course, I can't tell him the eagles told me. So I shrug.

"Yeah, well, the ecosystem took a huge hit. The food chain is out of whack. The mackerel gobbled up everything from minnows to zooplankton, then the big fish gobbled up all the mackerel. Now, the big fish have split to find food elsewhere. The ecosystem collapsed. Could take years to rebound."

Years? Gabriella and Merlin will starve by then. My stomach cramps.

Meanwhile, Cora is thinking hard. I can tell because her forehead is all scrunched up. She loves a mystery. Like in fifth grade, when our teacher Ms. Jones lost her cellphone connection. Cora figured it out right away: the cell tower up the street had been hit by lightning.

Cora catches me looking at her now. Her eyes narrow. She leans back against the VR cockpit.

"Watch out!" Will yells as the cockpit swings around the other way and almost hits her. She jumps out of the way, and her hand knocks a Post-it note off the handlebars. I lunge to help Cora, but pull myself back. Georgia is watching. Cora huffs and walks off. I step over and pick the Post-it note off the floor. Scribbled on the yellow paper are numbers and letters. Random, like a password. Maybe, it might get me access to Gabriella's GPS coordinates? I slip the paper into my pocket. Troy calls me over. Worried he's seen me, I tiptoe gingerly twirling my hair between my fingers.

"So, let me show you the dolphin," he says.

My heart jumps. "Yes," I say, but then Georgia walks over and I want to scream "No!"

Troy splashes the pool from the inside of the lab.

Nothing happens. "Let's go outside," he says. He leads us through the back door onto the deck. The round pool is thirty feet across.

"Wow. It's even bigger than your pool!" Avery says, gawking at Georgia, who winces, unimpressed.

Troy dips his hand into the water and splashes again. "Come on, girl." Finally, a fin pops up.

"Was she hurt?" I ask.

"Yep, got tangled pretty tight in those nets and was dehydrated." Troy then tells Ms. A how it was Frankie's father's boat and their nets that dragged the dolphin in.

The dolphin now swims over and pokes her snout up.

"Ew! Nasty." Georgia puts her hand over her mouth like she's about to throw up.

Across the dolphin's forehead is a three-inch gash, purple and gooey. Tears well up in my eyes.

"Right on her melon," Troy says.

"Her what?" Avery asks.

"It's how the dolphin sends sonar. And, sadly hers is damaged."

"Sonar? You mean like bats?" Will asks.

"Yeah. Dolphins, like bats, use echolocation to see their way in the dark."

"How's that work?" Cora asks.

"Dolphins use their melons to make a clicking sound. You and I can't *see* the sound, but it travels in waves. When the soundwave hits an object, it bounces back. That's the echo you hear. But dolphins sense it differently. The echo enters their lower jaws, then vibrates up through their inner ear. Nerves then send signals to their brain and a patterned message forms a 3D image. So, they can literally *see* the reef, the fish, or whatever else is up ahead in the dark."

"That's so jam!" Cora says, excited.

"It's a *superpower*!" Ms. A chimes in.

"And sometimes you can't even hear the dolphins' clicks because the frequency of the sound is too high for human ears to detect," Troy adds.

"Like a whistle that a dog can hear, but we can't?" Will asks.

"That's right!" Ms. A says, as she reaches her hand out to pet the dolphin, but it moves away.

Troy looks at me. "Why don't you try?"

"Huh?" I say.

"Yeah! Go on KeeRose." Georgia steps up beside me.

My stomach aches. I can barely breathe. Will wedges himself between us. Maybe he will protect me after all? He looks into the dolphin's eyes. "I bet she misses her mom," he says softly. Suddenly, his face turns ghost white.

I reach my hand out. The dolphin lets me pet her. "What's your name?" I say in a whisper so low I can barely hear myself.

"I don't remember," the dolphin whistles low.

"What about your pod?" I ask again in a whisper.

"What pod? Why does my head hurt?"

"You'll be fine. Just rest." I pet her cheek. My temples ring and throb. I shut my eyes. Darkness everywhere, then streaks of light, aqua blue, billow around me. I feel myself floating. Below lies a reef, and beyond it, a cave. But, it's all so misty.

"Is that her name?" Will whispers in my ear.

I didn't realize I said it aloud. I open my eyes. Georgia is craned around Will, watching me like a hawk. "Yo, what are you doing?" she asks.

"Uh, nothing. It's just bright outside." I squint and I reach for my cap.

"Oh, right, Camp Catalina. You really are a biology nerd, aren't you?" She smirks.

Ms. A announces we have ten minutes left before we have to board the bus.

"Come on, Avery." Georgia moves swiftly toward the door. "There's nothing here."

Misty dips low in the water.

My heart throbs. "Is she gonna be alright?" I ask Troy.

"I'm hoping in a couple weeks she'll get her sonar back. I mean there's no guarantee, but I'll be monitoring her progress," he says. "And, glad she's got a name now. Misty, right? Nice job."

I nod, but can't bring myself to tell him that Misty has amnesia. I don't want him interrogating me. I'm in enough trouble.

"I gotta go!" I blow Misty a kiss, and leave Cora and Will behind.

Back inside the lab, I search through the rows of aquariums, desperate to find something to partner with Georgia and Avery on. A tiger shark. A green sea turtle.

Mr. Bracket bounces over and pulls a compass out of his pocket. "Sharks and sea turtles—and many other fish—have an internal compass," he says. "They sense the Earth's magnetic field, just like this compass here. See the needle inside? That's a magnet." The red tip points to N, toward the North Pole. "That's how these animals navigate," he says.

"So they have a magnet inside their brain?" I ask.

"Well, kind of. How exactly animals sense the magnetic charge of the North and South Poles...well, that's a bit of mystery. Scientists are still figuring that part out."

That's cool. But Georgia and Avery barely listen. Time's running out. Finally, "Look!" I call out. "A peacock mantis shrimp." A sign by the tank reads *Danger! Stand back!* I put on my school scopes and read aloud: "Crustacean. Eats zooplankton." And whoa! There it is. Exactly what I remember! "Hey Georgia, check it out! 'At only ten centimeters long, this little green shrimp with red legs has the most powerful punch in the world!'"

"I already saw that!" Dante boasts, stepping beside me.

"Awesome! Well, I'm gonna take a video," Georgia says, and pulls out a camera drone the size of a golf ball. She's about to drop into the tank.

"Uh, I don't think that's such a good idea," I say, but she ignores me. *Plop*! The camera swims around. The shrimp's eyeballs rotate, tracking its every move.

I keep reading. "'The mantis shrimp has the most complex eyes in the animal kingdom. And, their two front claws have spring-loaded clubs to punch prey with the force of a twenty-two-caliber bullet!'"

The camera inches closer, and the shrimp punches suddenly. *Smash*! The camera breaks into a million pieces.

"Whoa!" Dillon shouts, joining us. "Wicked kick!"

"Rock star striker!" Georgia cheers. "I love the mantis shrimp! Great find, KyRose!"

What? She pronounced my name correctly! I can't believe it. I smile ear to ear!

On the bus ride back, Georgia invites me to sit with her and Avery. We're definitely going to be project partners. My mind drifts to the dresses hanging in my closet. Which one will I wear to her next party?

The sundress Abuela sewed for me is way too plain. I bet it doesn't even fit me anymore. Since I wore it last, I've grown at least two inches—today, it feels like three. Plus, it's out of fashion. I'm reminded of that sitting next to Tabeen. She straightens the pleats on her skirt as she clamors on and on about the spiders that she saw back at the Safe Haven. "You know the silk they spin for their webs? It's *bulletproof*! I can weave the grooviest Martian jumpsuit with it," she says with a big smile that shows off her dimples.

Rex sits in front of us holding up his finger, red and swollen like a sausage.

Rebecca leans across the aisle. "Hey, KyRose, did you see the electric eels? They pump these positive and negative electrolytes right inside their bodies. I'm gonna make battery packs for astronauts with gigabytes of power so they never run out of juice."

"Awesome!" I give her a high-five. Across my lap, my sketchbook is turned on. I already have two versions of the shrimp gizmo sketched out. Georgia shoots me a thumbs up from across the aisle. I smile. I'm so happy to be with the Primas. I wish the bus ride would never end.

I turn back, only once, to see Cora and Will sitting together. I feel a tinge of guilt, but mostly I'm relieved. Looks like Will found a partner. Now I have less to worry about. Right?

Ten

Howdy, Partners

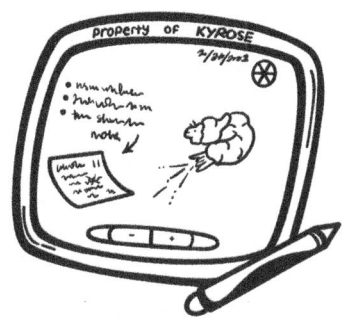

After the field trip, I stay up late to finish my sketches. I have seven versions of the Mantis Kicker, with levers both big and small. Georgia's bound to pick at least one of them. At ten o'clock, Sarafina turns off my lights and Wi-Fi. My head hits the pillow, but I can't sleep. I replay the day's events and smile in the dark. Yes! Georgia said my name *correctomundo*. Then, from the outer edges of my mind, I hear a faint whistle. Misty and that vision of drifting underwater comes back. It gnaws at me. But I know that Misty's in good hands. After all, Troy's the expert. He knows what to do. Which reminds me of Mom! What if she *does* give Troy the boot. Where would the Safe Haven go? Maybe Will got it all wrong. I mean, Troy never mentioned a thing. Outside of his messy desk, he seemed to have everything under control. I almost got the nerve to ask Mom at dinner, but I don't want to cause trouble.

My eyelids grow heavy. A second later, I sit up. Oh no! The password. I was so busy sketching, I forgot it in my jeans. Alfred will surely wash them in the morning. I might forget, so I pull myself out of bed. Fumbling in the dark, I find my jeans and tuck the Post-it note in the top drawer of my desk. I'll worry about tracking the eagles later. I plod back to bed. Who knows, with so little food on the island, maybe the eagles will move to Mexico, where there's plenty of food. Really, the farther the better, at least until soccer season ends. Abuela always said, wish for what you want. As I drift to sleep, I imagine my eagle friends flying into the sunset.

In the morning, I fling Georgia and Avery my sketches. All throughout the day, I ask them what they think. Each time, they say the same: "We'll look at 'em later." But the deadline to submit partners and animal superpowers is tomorrow!

When the bell rings, I race down the hall, hoping to get to practice early so I can ask them again. I turn the corner and bump into Will. My sketchpad tumbles to the floor, open to the screen with the spring-loaded gizmos.

He picks it up, glimpsing at the page.

I reach for the sketchbook. He pulls it away.

"So, partnering with Georgia, huh? Well, what about Misty? What did she tell you yesterday?"

"Nothing!" I say. Kids pass by us in the hall.

"Then how did you know her name?"

"I had a vision."

"Oh, so it's all in your head. You tricked me. You don't talk to animals. You're a phony. Just making fun of me!" He shoves the sketchbook at me.

"No! I wouldn't do that. It sucks to be made fun of," I say as Avery's snide Snow White nickname for me rings in my in head. "Misty has amnesia. It must be from when she got bumped in the head," I say, and tell him about the cave I saw. "Maybe it was a clue?"

"A clue to what?" Cora asks, suddenly walking up beside us.

I clutch the sketchbook tight against my chest. My bracelet zings. Practice starts in three minutes. "Gotta go!" I say.

"Sure, run off to your slave master," Cora says in a pissy tone. "Remember, I warned you."

"It's not like that. You'll see," I call out, sprinting past the trophy case.

Coach Hartley orders us to do four laps around the field to warm up. At the end of my first lap, I catch up to Georgia and Avery. I hear them talking about party dates.

"Hey," I say, panting. Neither of them looks over at

me, nor are they out of breath. "Uh, did you see the sketches? What do you think?"

"They're good. We'll use 'em. Thanks!" Georgia says casually.

"I can draw more?"

"No. It's okay," Georgia says. "Dante and Dillon will do the rest. They don't care if they crush boulders, balls, or VR bad guys. This project's gonna be a cinch with them as partners." She and Avery high-five.

"What? I thought we were gonna be—"

Avery cuts me off. "You can partner with Miriam." She smirks over her shoulder as we keep jogging.

Georgia chuckles. "Yeah, I hear she's cooking up some poop. Something about beetles being strong enough to roll their dung into a giant ball. I mean, really, she already stinks. Can you imagine?" The girls laugh and pick up the pace, leaving me in the dust. My heart drops to the ground. How could they be so mean? A part of me wants to pull their hair out.

Twenty minutes later, after a million jumps and sprints, I'm dying and not just of thirst. As I take a swig of water, I see Miriam over in the garden shoveling soil. If I partner with her, forget it! I can kiss goodbye any hope of ever being popular. I'd beg Tabeen and Rebecca, but they've already got partners teed up.

Coach Hartley blows her whistle. "Time to practice penalty kicks! Come on!"

I head out to the goal box as the rest of the team lines up at the yellow line. Georgia goes first of course! She kicks the ball right past me into the net. Doomed, I double over, my heart barely beating. Tabeen is up next. She smacks the ball with her cleat. The ball charges over my head and hits the goalpost. Baa-baa-boom! It echoes. Each girl takes a turn kicking. Bang. Boom. Thump. I listen to the echoes.

That's it! I know what to do! My mind plucks back over the dresses hanging in my closet. I'll wear the blue one with polka dots to Georgia's party.

When I get home, I race upstairs and holocam Cora.

"Uhh. Hey, listen," I say. "I'm sorry about all that stuff I said before. You know we'll always be best friends." I cross my fingers behind my back as I ask her, "Will you, please, be my partner on the class project? To build an echolocation vest? The astronauts could wear it to see in dark. I have sketches." I scribbled them down after practice. "I can throw 'em in a CAD program. We can 3D print them, and you can do the coding. What do you say?"

Cora stares at me blankly.

"Come on, pleazzze," I beg. "And Will would be brilliant at wiring it all up." I ping and join him to the cam, then go on pleading. "Who knows? Our vest could even win the GoMars competition." That perks Will up, but Cora remains silent. My mind races.

"What if we rig a version for Misty?" I say. "A kind of implant or something so she can have her sonar back!"

Will jumps in. "So she could swim again with her pod and her mom, once Troy releases her into the wild? That's it! I'm in," he says.

Cora's eyes light up. "Me too," she says, genuinely excited. I can tell 'cause her eyes are wide and sparkle, just like when she asks for two scoops of ice cream with sprinkles, please.

I sigh with relief.

When we hang up, I tell Sarafina to fling the sketches over to my new partners. But then, a sour taste fills my mouth and burns down to my chest, like when I lied to Mom about the game. I tell myself it's okay, it's just a tiny lie I told Cora and Will. I just didn't tell them my secret plan—that I'm going to wear the echolocation vest to be the best goalie in the world. With double vision—sight and sound—no ball will ever get past me. Move over, astronauts! I'll be best friends with Georgia in no time…and invited to all her parties.

Now, we just need to build the bloody gadget. How long could that take?

Eleven

Inventing

Sarafina wakes me up with marching orders. I jump out of bed, but first crank open the window. Beyond the speckled brown and orange autumn leaves that dangle from the trees, the sky is clear. Still no sight of Gabriella or Merlin, thank goodness! Here comes my delivery. The drone hovers outside the window. I tap my digi-bracelet. The package drops into my hand. Inside is a tube of Flawless lip gloss, currently trending on FriendZ's Hot List. I hope Georgia likes it. I've already gifted her a set of smart metallic tattoos and nail polish. Sarafina reminds, yet again, that I'm running low on LunaCoins. It's been two weeks since Cora, Will, and I started our project. The echolocation vest better be done today! And, it better work! Georgia's party is next

Saturday. She set the date and still hasn't invited me.

As I pack up my JellyGlobe, Puddles lays curled on my bed. Chin down like a pancake, he tracks my every move with love-hungry eyes.

"Can we pleazzze play when you get home?" He wags his tail.

"Sure, and I'm gonna need your help."

"You are?" He stands up, chest out. "How?"

Sarafina interrupts, "Your ShareCar arrives in three minutes and twelve seconds."

"I gotta go!"

"Humph!" Puddles snorts at the flowerpot speaker, then lies down. His ears droop.

"I'll show ya later. Promise," I say, and I better be right. I blow him a kiss and head out the door.

At school, just outside the FabLab, is this quote on the wall:

"To invent you need a good imagination and a pile of junk." —Thomas Edison

I walk into the FabLab. It hums with the churn and chatter of machines and kids fast at work. The room is still combined with the science lab into one big room. It'll be this way for three more weeks, until Exhibition Day. That's when we demo our final wares for friends and family. I look around the room. The front right corner is corded-off for Mars Mission Testing. Rebecca and her team are already there with their Eel Battery Pack. Lucky them! They get to pound, dig, and hike their way through a VR version of Mars. Of course, my secret plan is to take it to the real world.

Will waves me over. Clutching my bag, I head toward our table. Signs hang above each team's work station. I scoot around the Beetle Pushers and Turtle Navigators. No one looks at me. Everyone's busy, their heads down, assembling bits and pieces of their gadgets. Cora stands over by the circuit board station. Reprinting—again. After frying the other two boards and a near explosion, this one better work or I'm the one that's toast!

Across the room, Georgia and Avery burst out in laughter as Dante chases Dillon with their Mantis Kicker. It doesn't feel fair. That should be me over there having fun.

"Stop it, boys!" Ms. A quips.

They do, for a second…until she turns away to check on Tabeen and her team who are rapidly rolling spider fiber into balls of yarn. They grew it in a petri-dish, then moved it into a bio-reactor where it kept growing. Now it's in gallon-size buckets overflowing like cotton candy on steroids.

I slide past Rex as Mr. Bracket asks him how his

finger is doing.

"Better." Rex bends his knuckle up and down. Beside him is a 3D printer that oozes carbon fiber into yet another layer of his Snapper Beak. Guess Mabel made a lasting impression! Hinged together, the beak will act like a giant pair of pliers. Once the prototype is tested out, Rex says he'll make a final version out of graphene—a lightweight material that'll make the beak hardy enough to pluck gems from rocks and crack open all matters of Mars.

The *Echo Catcher* sign hangs above our work station. Splayed across the table is our vest. It's made of a plastic woven mesh. Will is hunched over, busy pinning twenty-two electrical nodes to the back side of the vest. Each node, the size of a blueberry, has a wire poking out. We need to connect these wires to the receiver that we already mounted on the front side of the vest.

Cora walks up. "Voila!" she says, snapping the new circuit board into the receiver. Will checks the connections, and then Cora uploads the code she's written onto the chip that lives inside the circuit board. I pick up the last piece of the puzzle. The emitter. It's basically a speaker the size of pistachio. I give it a squeeze. The emitter clicks just like the melon on a dolphin's head. But, of course, I can't hear the sound. Not at all. Because the frequency is too high: 150,000 hertz. Human ears can only hear 20 to 20,000 hertz. Still, when the sound waves bounce back, I'll be ready.

Biomimicry! Just like a dolphin. Instead of using our jaws and ears to catch sound waves, we use a different route—the vest. Our receiver is a sensor. It catches sound waves that bounce back—and not just from the emitter, but all sounds nearby. Our code then runs through a bunch of steps via an algorithm that Cora wrote up. It figures out the frequency and calculates distance, then signals corresponding nodes to pulse and vibrate. When I wear the vest, I'll feel the zings across my back. My nervous system will carry the signals to my brain. Neurons firing, new patterns forming. Ms. A said, after a few hours—or days or weeks—of practice, my brain will make sense of the patterns. Learn. Adapt. I'll be able to *see* sound waves, just like a dolphin echolocating. That's the theory, anyway. I can't wait to give it a whirl.

"Are you done yet?" I blurt, after watching Will fidget with the wires for a whole twenty minutes. It feels more like twenty hours. I then remind him and Cora, "You promised I could take it home to test it over the weekend! Right?"

"Yes, but hold on," Will says. "First, we have to finish it."

"Yeah, what's your hurry?" Cora asks.

I look away.

Will stands up. "I need to get the soldering iron to weld the nodes into place."

"I'll get it," I say popping out of my seat and reach for my bag.

On the way to the tool cabinet, I take a detour to Georgia's table.

"I got this for you," I say, handing Georgia the lip gloss.

"Are you kidding? Thanks!" She breaks it open and smears the wand across her lips, but still no invite to her party!

Ms. A walks over. Dante throws on his scopes and quickly acts busy reading aloud, "'The mantis shrimp can see a wide range of light frequencies. They have twelve photoreceptors and can see ultraviolet light. Butterflies, birds, reindeer, they too can see ultraviolet light. But not humans.'" Dante peeks over at Ms. A. She nods and walks off toward the next team. He then throws his feet onto the table. I find myself staring at his rainbow laces, then look up at the chart on the wall of the electromagnetic spectrum of light. There it is, clear as day: humans are limited! We can't hear all the sounds in the world, nor can we see all the light. But, what if we could?

I clear my throat. "Um…why don't you, uh, build some UV googles? So your Mantis Kicker can see ultraviolet light on Mars?"

Georgia's mouth drops open and her eyes grow wide. "Awesome idea!" she blurts.

I sigh with relief and smile. Hope floods in. My mind flashes to music pumping and me in my dress, spinning on the dance floor.

But it all stops when Dante rubs his neck and says, "Nu-uh. That's extra work!"

"No, it's not," Avery pounces. "KyRose can just *ask* that stupid shrimp how its eyeballs work. Right?" She smirks at me.

I shrug with a frown and wave my arms to show how ridiculous a suggestion that it!

"Don't worry. I'll figure it out," Dillon pipes up, "without talking to the shrimp, of course." He chuckles. "And hey, if we had goggles with our Kicker, we might win that GoMars contest."

"Shut up! I told you. We're not doing extra work!" Dante smacks him over the head.

Avery nods. Then her attention drifts, first to Ms. A then down to her bracelet to sneak a peek at her FriendZ feed.

Meanwhile, Georgia crosses her arms in defeat, not something she takes lightly, I know.

"I'll build them for you!" I hear myself say.

"Really? You'd do that for me? I mean, us!" Georgia stands and gives me a hug.

Wow! Now that should get me an invite to her

party! And it'll definitely be a solid back-up plan, should the echolocation vest be a bust. Thing is, I have no idea how to build a UV anything, much less goggles.

At the end of class, after I carefully tuck the finished vest into my backpack and Cora leaves, I turn to Will. Sheepishly I ask, "Uhh, can you do me a favor?"

Twelve
Trial & Error
... Adapting

When I get home, I put on the vest. I run to the bathroom and rifle through my drawer until I find a green headband to match my jersey. I sew a tiny pouch into the backside of the headband and slip the emitter inside. Carefully, I put on the headband and position the emitter so it's right above and between my eyes. On my Third Eye. That where Abuela said we can see inside ourselves. I take a deep breath. I hope this works. Abuela said the Third Eye is also where we connect to *The Zone* and tune in to the "vibrations" of the universe. Perfect for my emitter! Just hope my signals don't get crossed.

I power up the emitter, along with the vest. Sound waves bounce—off the walls, the toilet, the sink. I can tell, because nodes on the vest buzz in a crazy sequence across my back. *Di-dah, bi-bah, bi-dah, di.* Thing is, I don't see anything different. To be sure, I tie a bandana over my eyes. Blind as a bat, I sit and wait for my brain to kick in—to learn the patterns and make sense of it all. I fumble down the hall. Knock my nose. Stub my toe. *Ouch*! *Ow*!

All the next day, Saturday, I wander in the dark, bumping and bruising. At dinner, I refuse to take off the vest or the blindfold.

"Catch any echoes yet?" Dad asks. "Can you see me?" I know he's leaning close, because I smell the garlic on his breath.

"No!" I slam my fork down onto the table. Three nodes flash hot on my back. How do dolphins do this? When Dad and I went surfing this past summer, a pod of dolphins had cruised by us. I heard clicks. I didn't know then that it was a tool. I paddled up beside one of the dolphins. He had speckled marks up by his spout and let me rub his jelly-tight skin.

"Hey saw you ride that wave. Not bad!" the dolphin said and winked at me. He then spun up in a somersault. "Guess I better catch up to my pod. See you later," he said, and swam off.

By Sunday morning, still in the dark, I'm ready to

give up. I pray Will has had better luck making those goggles. I'm about to cam him when Jack shouts, "Hey, catch!" I still have my blindfold on, but whip around and grab the ball racing towards me. I *see* it! And everything. Walls, windows, floors…and Jack. They all come into view. I bounce over and give Jack a kiss on the cheek. "My brain's adapting!"

"Pretty cool, li'l sis," he says, and musses my hair. I don't even mind.

I comb the house, duck through doorways, and weave around the dining room table. I can *see* Alfred vacuuming, gobbling cushions off the sofa, and Dad's blender grinding in the kitchen. But the true test is still ahead. I wait for Mom and Dad to go for a walk, and for Jack to skate off to meet up with Emily. That's when Puddles and I head out to the alley to play soccer. With my eyes still covered, Puddles kicks and nudges the ball. He even lobs it with his head. I catch it, again and again.

"Hurray. 98% success," Sarafina applauds. "The astronauts will likely enjoy your invention!"

"I don't care about that," I say. "It's tomorrow's game against the Cubs that counts. I'm not letting them score…not once."

"Wait!" Sarafina says. "You're going to wear the vest? During the game?"

"Yes! Of course."

Two seconds pass. She comes backs. "I just read the entire Sports League Handbook. Wearables are against the rules."

"I know that!"

"Well, then don't you think it's a bad idea?"

"No! Win the game. Go to Georgia's party. It's perfect."

"Well, I can't help you." She huffs.

"What do you care? You're just a computer. Plus, don't you have to follow my every command? Isn't that written in some code?" I put my hands on my hips. "As long as no one gets hurt, right?"

"Well, that *is* how I am programmed!"

"So butt out. And don't tell Mom."

Puddles and I keep playing. I take my blindfold off. I have double vision: *sight* and *sound*. I feel #invincible.

That evening, I fling Cora to tell her the vest is jam. She sends back a thumbs-up emoji.

I then cam Will. He sits at a workbench beneath a spotlight. Beside him is a wooden chest. I tell him the scoop—the vest works like a charm. He doesn't say a thing about trying to win the GoMars competition. Which is fine with me. I get to the point and ask him how the UV goggles are coming along.

"I'm almost done. Take a look." He holds up two blue tinted lenses. One is darker than the other and they're set in red frames held together by a rubber strap. Will slips them on.

"Whoa. So Amelia Earhart. You planning to fly over the Atlantic?" I ask.

"Yeah." He laughs. "As long as the plane doesn't crash in the water." He then sneers and his lip curls, but he shakes it off. "Anyway, the goggles are even cooler when you look through 'em." Will stares across the room. "I can see sparks on the light switches, and earlier, I had a ripe, yellow banana that glowed blue. I'd show you, but I got hungry and ate it."

"Where did you get all the stuff to make the goggles?" I ask.

"I had them."

"You did? Just laying around?"

"Yeah. From old camera equipment." He pulls the goggles off and his eyes slip to the chest sitting beside him.

"Why do you have old camera stuff?"

"It was my mom's."

"Oh, she's a photographer?"

"She was." His voice dips.

"What do you mean was?" I ask, and it dawns on me.

"I don't talk about it," he says in a fluster. "But fine. If you need to know, she died!"

"Oh, I'm so sorry. Was she sick?"

"No." He shakes his head. "It was late spring. We lived on the lake back in Illinois. My mom took the boat out. She, um, loved to take pictures at sunset." Will pauses. "She asked me to come with her that day, but I...I wanted to go swimming instead." He shakes his head. "*It* happened on her way back. It was dark. The boat hit a log and flipped. She...." Will shivers. "I told you, I don't want talk about it." His eyes fill with tears. Mine too. "I hate the water! Scares the hell out of me," he says.

"Thanks for telling me...about your mom," I say softly.

Will punches the table with his fist. "I should have been there on that boat with her. I could have saved her!"

"It's not your fault," I say, but Will looks away.

That night I lie in bed. My eyelids grow heavy. The next thing I know, the wind is blowing. My throat is dry. I can't breathe. Orange smoke hangs over the field. From a mountain of bleachers, fans cheer. Their feet pound on metal floorboards, like a drumroll. My heels burn with blisters and my hair whips my cheeks. Between strands, I see Georgia glaring at me. Coach Hartley shakes her head and crosses her arms. The chanting grows louder and louder. "Chea-ter! Chea-ter!"

I look down. No jersey. I'm only wearing my underwear…and the vest!

"Chea-ter! Chea-ter!"

The ball flies over my head. I duck, spin, and fall. *Thump*! I lay on the ground.

Someone is licking my face. Sobbing, I open my eyes. It's Puddles. He's licking my tears away. I'm on the floor in my room. It's still dark out.

The next morning, when I wake up, I'm still on the floor. Puddles is curled up beside me. I remember the nightmare, and my heart begins to race. I jump up and put on the vest. Over it, I put on a tee. Then, I put on another layer, then a third, and a fourth. I wear my soccer jersey over it all and look in the mirror. Satisfied, I peel the layers and vest off and stuff them into my JellyGlobe backpack.

Downstairs, I dip into the kitchen. JellyGlobe on my back, I'm anxious to go. Dad offers me a plate of scrambled mung beans.

"No, thanks. Just juice," I say. "Two bottles, please." I shoot him a cutesy smile. "Oh, and can I get that new blend you got, with over 3,000 likes? Definitely tastes good, right?" I don't want Georgia to spit it out.

"The Energizer. It's delicioso!" Dad says, holding up the bottles, double-fisted. "Plum and peppermint with green tea extract."

"No nuts. Right?" I ask, suddenly petrified I'll send

Georgia into anaphylactic shock—her throat closing up, almost dying. That would not be good for me! Especially on a game day.

"Nada. No nuts, just fermented ginger. I slipped it in. You know—mucho good for the tum." He pats his belly.

"Hey, Santa Claus." Jack glides into the kitchen. "Feeling generous? Could I use the back alley of the juice shop after school this week? Em and I are shooting another video."

"Sure," Dad says, "but today I won't be there 'til later. I'm going to your sister's game."

"Me too." Mom pokes her head in.

"What? You're coming to see me play? Today?" I feel dizzy…about to faint. "No!" I blurt.

Mom and Dad frown obviously confused.

"Come to my game next week, instead, please," I say, batting my lashes as hard as I can. "I need more practice. I want to impress you guys." I figure by then, I'll be an expert Echo Catcher. That, or be kicked off the team!

I sprint past Coach Hartley. The last thing I need is her interrogating me about why I'm wearing so many layers under my jersey. Back in the locker room, I must have checked my headband and jersey twenty-five times to be sure the emitter and vest are totally hidden.

As I run to the goal box, nodes zing across my back.

I glance up at the treetops. A shadow stirs. Oh no! Gabriella and Merlin. They're back. I'm so stupid. I never tried that password. I totally forgot about it. I could have been tracking them this whole time. There's more bobbing in the branches. I notice it's just a family of ravens. Phew!

Arms wide, I guard the goal with my life. Two minutes in, I'm sweating. Nodes dance across my back. The ball spins and the Cubs charge. Usually, I adore baby bears, but not today. Today, they're my enemy.

The emitter tucked into my headband clicks. Sound waves ripple. They bounce off players suited in jerseys, and clad in shin guards and metal cleats. But I have double vision and can see it all. Every corner, every kick. The ball sails over Rebecca, past Tabeen. I track the arc. Sensors zinging, I jump up and catch the ball! Again and again.

"Way to go, KyRose!" Georgia shouts. I kick the ball back to her each time. She sprints and scores. Her mom shouts from the bleachers, "You're number one!" Georgia beams tall. Everything's going my way.

Cora and Will wave at me from the stands. Maybe I should've told them the truth? I tug at the vest, making sure it's hidden. The strap cuts into my ribs. I must have cinched it too tight. I'll live with the pain. The prize is worth it.

The whistle blows. Game over. Jaguars win, 3-0. Our

fans cheer, and my teammates jump in celebration. Georgia runs over. "Great game. Wow! So, wanna come to my party?!"

"Yes!!" My plan worked. Popularity, here I come.

Georgia reaches to give me a hug, but I flinch. She cocks her head with a baffled look.

I fan my armpit. "I stink," I say. Which is true, but my heart is racing. What if she had felt the vest under jersey? Even with all the layers, I can't risk it. I'm heading to the locker rooms to get changed when Rex skips past Georgia and up to me.

"KyRose! Stellar moves! You're a star in the making."

"Really?" I let out a nervous giggle.

"Yeah, even the twins couldn't keep up with you on *Smash Spectator*. No one could. Here, take a look. I streamed the game." He replays it from his bracelet. "And, I posted it on FriendZ. It's already got 649 likes!" I watch as the number jumps to 686…712…880.

"Whoa! That's because of me?"

"Yeah," Rex says. "Quick, give me a quote."

"Like what?"

"How did it feel? Where did you learn those moves?" he asks.

"Practice," I say.

"Must have been a lot. What? Have you been playing since you were like two years old?"

I giggle. Of course, I can't tell him the truth.

"Uh…Go Jaguars!" I say, figuring that's safe. Won't give my secret away.

In the locker room, Georgia hustles over. "What was that with Rex?"

I tell her.

"Oh. You know," she says, stepping close. "As captain, it's my job to give all the interviews. So, if Rex asks you again for a quote, tell him you have nothing to say. Got it?"

"Uh, okay."

"Good!" She shimmies her shoulders. "Now, tell me…whatcha going wear to my party?"

I'm so excited I can barely breathe. I hope the blue polka dot dress looks alright. But then I think of Cora. What if I could actually get Georgia to invite her to the party too?

Thirteen
Mission Possible

On Thursday, Will finally meets me at my locker.

"Sorry it took so long." He fumbles with the goggles. "Just wanted to make sure they wouldn't fall apart."

I slip them into my bag. Avery watches from across the hall.

In the FabLab, I go to demo our vest. I stroll into the Mars Mission Testing area and put on the augmented/virtual reality headset. I select *Mission 1* and enter the red planet. The vest tingles across my back. As I walk through a dark tunnel, I jump over pools of lava. I survive. No problem. On to *Mission 2*, I cruise through a sand storm back to base station.

Mission complete! "Great job!" Will says.

During a class break, after everyone's left the room,

Will and Cora decide to show Ms. A what I can do. They slide chairs, stools, and tables around to setup a "real world" obstacle course. Then, they blindfold me so I definitely can't cheat and call Ms. A over to watch as I easily walk around the furniture.

"Very impressive!" Ms. A says. "KyRose, you're highly adaptable!" I take a bow.

"Maybe we'll win that GoMars contest after all?" Will says under his breath.

"Oh, yeah, KyRose has got *abilities*." Cora winks. "It's a wonder she even needs the vest to echolocate." She and Will applaud. I take another bow and blush. Then suddenly, I feel nauseous. Why am I lying to my friends? I should tell them the truth! But, Will, he'll worry I'll get caught. And Cora, well, she'll kill me if she finds out I've been breaking school rules just to impress Georgia. Maybe after the party I can tell them the truth—if Cora gets to come with me that is. 'Cause then she'll see how it's all been worth it.

"Is everything okay?" Cora asks.

I swallow and pull off the blindfold. That's when I realize she's talking to Ms. A, not me. Our teacher's eyes are strained. Her scopes rest on the tip of her nose.

"I was just reading a message from Troy," she says. "Bad news, I'm afraid. That dolphin at the Safe Haven...."

"Misty?" I pop up on my toes. "Is she okay?"

"She's worse. Not eating. Troy says her echolocation hasn't come back. He now thinks the damage might be permanent. And if it is, she'll never be able to survive in the wild, not without sonar. And, they haven't found her pod yet either."

"Oh no!" Cora says.

"She'll be an orphan," Will moans, and gazes out the window. A second later, as though struck by lightning, he bolts up and looks straight at me. "We've got to help her! Remember? You said we could build her an implant."

"I did?" I stutter.

"Don't worry. We'll figure out a way!" Cora says, ever the optimist. "Remember, Mr. Bracket said lots of tech made for space travel is used here on Earth. We can do this!"

I know! I'm doing it now, I want to shout aloud. Why else would Georgia invite me to her party and kids on FriendZ ever notice me? The video Rex posted has over 53,462 likes last I checked!

"We have to go see Troy," Will says.

"Today, after school," Cora adds.

"I'll meet you there after practice," I say, suddenly regretting that I never checked on Misty during these past few weeks.

"Bravo! I'm really proud of you kids," Ms. A says. "Solving problems. Helping others. I'll tell Troy you're coming."

Will nods with a bit of confidence, and Cora puts her arm around me. I guess now we really are on a mission!

After class, the vision I had when I met Misty haunts me. Maybe it was a clue and we *can* somehow find her pod. When the bell rings, instead of going to lunch, I head to the library. It's empty—even the librarian has gone to eat. I walk past the small display of printed paperbacks shelved in a glass case, like in a museum. The main section of the library is filled with cubicles for reading and watching e-books. This is where I sat last week reading *Delphus & Friends*, the novel Mr. Bracket and Ms. A assigned me, Cora, and Will to read. The story is about five kids in ancient Greece who meet a dolphin. In it, I read how ancient Greeks protected dolphins and gave them rights, like humans. Dolphins were known to save sailors from drowning. They'd swim the sailors to shore when their ships ran aground or sank during a storm, and if any human ever killed a dolphin, they would go to jail.

Past the cubicles is the reference section. Here, I choose an A/VR station by the window. I slip on the headset. "Search geology, Channel Islands," I command. Abuela always told me that stones—like the ringlets in a tree trunk—tell us the stories of the past. I watch as the MetaTech logo loads onto the screen. A view of planet Earth spins from outer space. It then zooms in to the Pacific Ocean, and down further to California and the eight islands that lay sprinkled off the coast. A voice speaks, "Fourteen million years ago, the tectonic plates shifted. The plates rubbed up against each other, and the earth's crust began to thin. Volcanoes erupted and the Channel Islands were born with rocky shores, mountains, canyons and sea caves."

Caves! I knew it!

Just as I put the headset away, I hear a knock on the window behind me.

"It's her! It's her!"

I spin around. Gabriella is pecking on the window pane.

Quickly, I scan the library. It's still deserted, so I slide the window open.

"I told you we'd find her," Gabriella boasts, puffing her chest. She looks thinner than when I saw her last. Both the eagles do. Merlin lands on the windowsill beside her.

"You can't be here. I'll get caught. You'll ruin everything," I say. "What? Are you hungry? Is that it?" I check my pockets. They're empty.

Merlin squawks. "I told you. She doesn't want to see us."

Gabriella tells me the dolphins never came back.

"We searched all the islands. Now I have no one to hunt with, and with so few mackerel…." She begins to cry.

"Leave the island or you'll starve." I tell them what Troy said. How the ecosystem needs time to recover.

"But Catalina is our home," Gabriella says. "We have the perfect nest up on the cliffs. We've even heard songs, of late, echoing from the air shafts that surround our nest—I think it's a sign from Mother Nature to stay put and wait it out. If we only had enough food."

"And if we were to flee," Merlin adds, "any place we go, we'd have to fight other eagles, osprey, and even red-tailed hawks, to win new territory." He tips his wing. "It would be dangerous."

I let out a sigh. "Maybe the mackerel—and the food chain—will recover sooner than Troy thinks. I can ask him." I try and sound hopeful.

"Oh, thank you!" Merlin wraps his wing around Gabriella.

My heart warms. "Oh, and if the pod does come back, please let me know." I tell them about Misty and how she's going to need her pod.

"We will, dear," Gabriella says, then turns to Merlin. "See, we knew you cared."

Just then, the library door swings open. "Someone's coming. I've gotta go!" I say, and slam the window shut.

The cafeteria is filled with chatter. I head straight

toward Will and Cora to tell them about the sea caves and how Gabriella and Merlin said that Misty's pod isn't around any of the islands. But as I pass Georgia's table, she waves me over. "Sit here!" she points. Tabeen scoots over with her bowl of tabbouleh and chopped peppers to make room for me. I guess I have no choice. My news to Will and Cora will have to wait. I take a seat.

"Ew, what's that?" Georgia stares at Rebecca's plate. It smells of sweet saffron.

"This is my mama's jambalaya," Rebecca says, and starts humming.

"Please, don't sing me a song about it!" Georgia says.

I work up my nerve and pull the goggles out of my bag. I hope it's enough to ask for the favor I need! I hand them to Georgia.

"Ah, the UVs. With red frames!" She shimmies her shoulders, then grabs and dangles them on her finger, showing Dante and Dillon at the next table over. "Hey, guys! KyRose did it! She made 'em!"

Avery narrows her eyes, glaring at me.

"Let me try 'em," Dillon says.

"No, me first!" Dante grabs for the goggles. Georgia pulls them away, then tosses the goggles right between the twins, who clamor over them like piranha.

"Give it to me!"

"Mine!"

The twins roll onto the floor. A crowd gathers. The

Primas burst out into laughter.

That's when I lean over to Georgia. "Uh, so I was wondering if I could bring someone to your party?"

"Who? Your brother? Sure, he's definitely invited."

"Uh, no." I clear my throat, ready to say it's actually Cora but then hear—

Snap! and Dillon yell, "*Ouch!*" as he rubs his knuckles.

"You idiots! Give me that!" Georgia scolds. "Now what are we gonna do? The lenses are all scratched up."

"I can fix it," Dillon says, pulling himself off the floor.

"Shut up, stupid!" Dante trips his brother. "I'll do it!"

Georgia then looks at me, batting her lashes. "Do you mind?" She holds out the goggles.

"Uh, sure." I take them from her, then glance over at Will. He and Cora are still sitting together finishing their lunch.

"Oh, and who is it? That you want to bring to the party?" Georgia asks.

"Uhhh, never mind," I cower, abandoning ship. I have no idea if Will can fix the goggles by Saturday. Maybe I'll just have to come up with a new plan.

Fourteen
My Pod or Yours

After practice, I head to the Safe Haven to meet Cora and Will. As the ShareCar steers past Oyster Village, twenty-foot-long cranes pump concrete to lay out the foundation. Looming behind them on the waterfront, giant 3D printers wait their turn to build the walls for the restaurants and shops. Mom stands by a fence. She wears boots and a yellow hardhat. Beside her are two crewmen. They study a set of drawings and point to the other side of the fence at the Safe Haven.

Cora and Will are already in the lobby.
"Did you bring the vest?" Will asks.
I pull it out of my bag.
"Why is it wet?" Will grimaces.

"Oops, my water bottle must have leaked." I reach back into my bag and pretend to tighten the top of my bottle, then I step away and wipe the sweat off on my neck. Most of it's already dry, evaporated.

"Sarafina," I whisper. "Remind me to pack a towel for practice from now on."

"Sure thing," she answers into my earbud.

With his lab coat wrinkled and his hair askew, Troy walks in. "Hey, kids." He seems as if he hasn't slept or showered in days. "Jenha—I mean, Ms. A." He straightens his collar. "She said you had something for Misty? I've tried everything."

"We built this. It's for our Mars project." Will holds up our vest. I demo it.

"Wow! It really works!" Troy says, surprised.

"We think we can build a version for Misty, a kind of implant," I say, looking over at Cora.

"Yeah, I've got a couple ideas." Cora adjusts her scopes.

"Definitely worth a try! Come on." Troy leads us toward the back. On the way, I hear a squawk.

"I'll meet you there," I say, and duck inside the rainforest.

"Kyy-Ros-za! You are back. Squawk!" Mabel spreads her wings. A rainbow of color brightens the room. I smile and scratch her neck. She coos.

"My brothers and sisters, we used to rub each

131

other's necks all the time. Oh, how I mizz them."

"You really *do* want to go back to the jungle, don't you?"

Mabel coos louder. "I dream of it every night."

My heart flutters. Maybe, after we help Misty, we can get Mabel back home. I skip down the hall and into the ocean biome just as Troy splashes the pool. Misty swims over slowly. Her ribs poke against the thin layer of her blubber. Troy tells us she's lost sixty pounds—that's 10% of her body weight. A crusty scab covers the gash across her melon. Misty nudges closer.

I wait for Troy to walk off to his desk with Cora and Will. He shoves over a pile of papers, and they lay out the vest and start chatting about waterproof fabric options. With Troy safely out of earshot, I turn and in a soft voice say, "Hello, Misty. You don't mind if I call you that, right? Or, maybe now you remember your real name?"

"No, I don't, but I like Misty, and I like you too. You never told me your name." She brushes her fin against my hand. I tell her. "There is something I remember," she says. "I was caught in the nets. A friend, or maybe he's my cousin, was trying to free me. But he couldn't." Jelly-like tears swell in her eyes, and she tips her snout.

"Well, what if we could set you free? And find your pod? Would that cheer you up?" I ask.

Misty flaps her flippers. "Yes!"

I explain how the vest works as I hear snippets of Cora and Will chatting about tacking on the emitter without hurting her. "You'll have sonar again," I tell her. "I can train you. But first, you need to eat to gain your strength."

She opens her mouth. I throw her a fish from a bucket. She swallows it and asks, "My pod? Are they far away?"

"Hey, you got her to eat!" Troy says, suddenly standing beside me.

My heart pounds. What if he heard me talking to her? I pretend he didn't. "We need to find her pod," I say. "You tagged some of the dolphins this summer, right?" Gabriella and Merlin might have lost track of them, but Troy couldn't, not with his tech.

"I did tag the dolphins, but for some reason, the signals on their trackers aren't coming in." He looks up at the monitors.

"Could it be they're out of range?" I ask.

"An entire network of satellites orbit Earth tracking those signals. There's no way they wouldn't pick it up unless the dolphin swam somewhere deep. But still, they have to come up for air. It's probably a malfunction of the nanochips on their tattoos." Troy strokes his goatee with a baffled look.

"Well, what about your friend Frankie? He's out fishing all the time. Maybe he's seen the pod?" I ask.

"We can't let Misty down. She wants to be free."

"And how do you know that? Did she tell you herself?"

"Yes!" I blurt. It just comes out.

"Ah ha! I knew it. You *can* talk to animals." Troy points at me with his mouth agape. I cower, ashamed. But then he says, "It's amazing! KyRose, you have a special gift. A superpower all your own!"

"Really?" I never thought of it as a *superpower*.

"Yes, now let's use it. What else did Misty tell you?"

I tell them about her amnesia.

"I bet she'll remember everything as soon as she sees her mom again," Will says, joining us with Cora. "We can't let her be an orphan!" He kicks the edge of the pool. Then suddenly, a howling wind blows in under the windows and swirls inside the lab.

Troy cams Frankie. He and his father's holograms appear life-size in the lab. In actuality, they're on the deck of their boat. Catalina looms behind them in the horizon.

"Hey, Frankie," Troy says, "and Captain Maloney, How's it going?"

The captain lifts his tattered cap, showing his gray hair tucked beneath. "No fish. Bum knee. Couldn't be better!" the old man scoffs, then wipes his brow under the hot sun with the back of his leathery hand.

"Pops, come on. Take a load off," Frankie says,

offering him a seat on a torn cushion. He props the captain's leg up on a rusty crab trap.

Troy then tells Frankie how we're students of Ms. A's, about the vest, and how we're going to try and use it on Misty. "It's a pretty slick invention—right up your alley, Frankie," Troy says.

"Nice to meet you, kids!" Frankie says. "Happy to help however I can."

"Well, have you seen Misty's pod?" Will asks. "She'll never be able to find them on her own." Will tells him about her amnesia.

"How do you know *that*?" Frankie asks leaning in.

Troy tells him I talk to animals. Frankie raises his eyebrows. I grit my teeth. They better not tell anybody else.

"So you're sure Misty can't remember, not a thing, huh?" Frankie slips his hands into his pockets.

Will glances at me.

"Sorry, but that pod's long gone," Frankie says. "Probably down to Mexico by now. Or even as far as Hawaii. Ain't that right, Pops?"

Misty slaps her tail in the pool.

"Yeah, last we seen 'em was just north of here," the captain says, "on the other end of the island. Same place we caught that dolphin in our nets. Damn mackerel, damn overfishing. Of course, the pod's gone. But we had a good run over summer, didn't we, Francis? You pointing that gadget of yours. Schools of fish were practically jumpin' into our boat."

"What gadget?" Will asks. "Was it a radar gun?"

"Not quite," Frankie says. "It's something I've been tinkering with since I was about your age."

"You know, Frankie also went to school at MakerX20," Troy adds.

"Well, sure is a shame the fish ran out," the captain grunts. "Ain't it?"

"Don't worry, Pops. We're still gonna have enough money to buy that fish farm you've always wanted."

"Oh yeah, sure we are." The captain rolls his eyes, and sighs. He then sits back and pulls a sandwich out of a cooler.

"Hey, Troy, when will the mackerel be back?" I think about Gabriella and Merlin starving and tell them about the eagles.

"Well, I did hear over the radio," Frankie interrupts, "that some of the fishing boats have already sighted mackerel near some of the islands further north."

"Really?" A sense of relief washes over me. The eagles just might be able to stay and keep their nest.

"So then, what are we doing here?" the captain asks. "Let's start the engine and get out there."

"Hold up, Pops. Like you said, overfishing isn't cool. I learned that the hard way. Troy, what do you think—when will it be okay to fish for mackerel again?"

"Not 'til the numbers are high enough to sustain the local ecosystem. Look, I'll tell you what," Troy says. "I've got a ton of bills and forms from the city that I gotta get through." He looks at the pile of papers on his desk. "They've got me jumping through hoops. I'm way behind. Frankie, how about I give you access to our computers and ROVs? Analyze the data with our A.I. Share it with us and then you'll also know exactly when there'll be enough to fish."

"Consider it done," Frankie says. He cups his hand to his cheek, so the captain can't hear. "*Psst*," he says. "Truth is...I hate to eat fish!"

We chuckle and Frankie winks.

Just before Troy ends the call, I ask, "Know of any sea caves out there?"

"Caves?" Frankie coughs. "Nope. Why do you ask?"

"Just a hunch."

When we hang up, I pull Cora and Will over to the holographic tabletop with the map of the ocean floor. I swipe my thumb and forefinger over the vectors of light and zoom in on Catalina. As the pixels recalibrate, jagged cliffs come into view. The island dips, like a cone, deep into the ocean and spreads its tendrils out, weaving into a valley of reefs.

"Look! There!" I gasp. Will and Cora lean in. "That could be a cave." I snap a photo of the coordinates to check out later with Sarafina.

137

As we're about to leave, Troy holds up the vest. "Well, thanks. I'll keep this to make a version for Misty."

"No!" I blurt out. That's mine! My palms break into a sweat.

"Why? We don't need it," Cora says casually. "Exhibition Day's not for two more weeks."

But that's not what's important. I have practice tomorrow and more games before playoffs begin.

"Mr. Bracket wants us to keep testing, you know, to make improvements." It's all I can think to say. "I need it back. I mean, we need it back."

"Come on Saturday, in the afternoon around 5:30," Troy says. "I'll be done feeding the animals. Hopefully, I'll have made a dent in these papers as well. I'll show you what I've come up with for an implant. And you can have the vest back then."

"Sure," Cora says. "We don't have anything. Right?" She turns to me and Will.

"Uh, well," I stutter. "I have to, uh…." I cross my fingers behind my back. "I promised my mom that I'd help her around the house," I say.

Sarafina chatters in my ear, "I don't see that on your calendar. Only, Georgia's party at six o'clock."

"Shush!" I flip my head, pretending to sneeze.

"Bless you," Troy says.

"Can't you help your mom on Sunday, instead?" Cora asks.

"Uh, my mom…she's working on Sunday," I say. Total lie.

I run over to Misty and blow her a kiss. "I'll be back soon," I promise, even though it won't be on Saturday. Then while Cora's over inspecting the VR cockpits wearing her scopes, I slip Will the scratched-up UV goggles. He says he can make a new pair by tomorrow, since he's already made them once. But really, it doesn't matter. I couldn't ask Cora to come with me to the party anyway. Now, I just have to keep up the lie.

Fifteen

Sirens of Fame

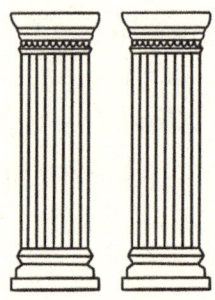

The next day, I fake a stomach ache to get out of practice. Without the vest, I can't risk looking like a fool. Georgia might uninvite me from the party just like that. So I hand her the new goggles and sit on the bench.

On Saturday afternoon, there are four dresses splayed out on my bed. "What about this one, Puddles?" I hold up the blue polka dot dress. It's identical to the one Avery just posted on FriendZ.

"I love circles. They remind me of balls," Puddles says. "Wear it and everyone will want to play with you." But if Avery wears the same dress, we'll both look stupid, and she'll hate me forever.

"How about this instead?" I hold up the rose taffeta mini dress with an origami collar and sash pocket.

"Wow!" Puddles says, panting. "But, really, you'd look good in anything."

I pat him on the head. My digi-braclet zings.

Before I even look, Sarafina tells me it's Cora. I drop the dress and accept the cam.

"So, did you get your stuff done?" Cora asks.

"Uh. What stuff?"

"I thought you were helping your mom?"

"Oh. Yeah, right. I am." It comes out awkwardly.

"What are those dresses for?" Cora's eyes shift down. I tilt my wrist up.

"Oh, my Mom's got me trying on old clothes. Part of the spring cleaning thing we're doing," I say.

"But it's only fall," Cora says. "Are you okay?"

"I'm fine."

"Well, if you do finish early, come by the Safe Haven," she says.

"Alright, but if I don't," (and I know I won't!) "be sure to grab the vest and bring it to school on Monday! Okay?"

We end the call. I decide on the pink dress, then take a few selfies. Of course, I don't post them. Which reminds me. "Hey, Sarafina. Turn off GPS on my bracelet."

"Why?" she asks.

"Just do it."

Downstairs, Mom is on the sofa wearing her scopes. She thumbs through what seems like a set of virtual drawings. She sketches here, then makes notes there with her finger.

"Bye. See you later," I say.

"Where are you going?"

"I told you. Georgia's having a party."

"Oh, right," Mom says. "Sorry, I've got my nose in this permit thing."

"I thought you got all your permits?" I ask.

"All but one," Mom says. "Mr. Sphinx insists that we expand the property. We're taking over the neighbors on the south side."

"So it's true! You're kicking the Safe Haven out."

"Well, I wouldn't quite say it like that."

"Mom, that's where Troy works…and where Misty is right now."

"Oh, you know Troy. Who's Misty?" Mom pulls off her scopes and actually looks at me. "Is Misty a *friend* of yours?" She tips her head. "Human or animal? Honey, we talked about this."

"No, *you* talked about it."

Mom rolls her eyes. "Where's Cora, by the way? I haven't seen much of her lately. Is she going to the party too?"

"Uhh! No!" I stammer.

Sarafina pokes me with a haptic and my bracelet

squeezes around my wrist. It's 5:47. I can't be late. Georgia told me not to miss the jugglers.

"Just—never mind." The last thing I need is to tell Mom about Cora right now. "I gotta go. I'm gonna take a MagBoard and you can pick me up later. Okay? Or just send a car whatever." I run for the door and bump into Alfred. He spins around, nearly dropping the tray of cucumber sandwiches and a pot of tea.

"Take a jacket," Mom calls out. "It'll be chilly tonight." I yank a sweater off the hook. I can't get sick, of course, or she'll miss work unless Dad can stay home and take care of me.

"The temperature is forecasted to drop to fifty-six degrees Fahrenheit," Sarafina says into my ear.

"Yeah, yeah, but it's gonna look stupid over my dress," I say. Outside, I stash the sweater in the bushes near the edge of the lawn. As I do, I startle a lizard who scurries off. My heart lurches…what if Mom shuts down the Safe Haven? What'll happen to Misty and Mabel and all the other animals? But I can't worry about it. Not now. I jump on the MagBoard. I've got a party to go to!

Halfway to Georgia's, the streets get wider and the houses bigger. I turn on Elm Way. The sun on my cheek flickers.

"Wait up!" It's Gabriella, with Merlin right on her tail. The eagles glide like a single arrow shooting through the sky, aimed at my heart.

I press my hands over the pink taffeta, but the eagles don't seem to notice my dress. They struggle to flap their wings, but I can't slow down. I'll be late. Gabriella reaches me first, huffing and puffing. She calls back to Merlin, "Stay behind me and *draft*. I'll resist the wind for both of us. Save your energy." She then asks me anxiously, "What did Troy say? Are the mackerel back?"

"Good news." I tell her about the spotting of fish around the other islands. "It's just a matter of time 'til Catalina will have plenty of mackerel again."

"But, how long?" Merlin asks. His voice trembles.

I tell them how the ROVs are counting fish, so we can chart the number and see the growth rates. "You'll be the first to know, I promise. Hopefully, the dolphins will be back too…for Misty's sake."

"We'll keep an eye out for the pod. We need them as much as she does," Gabriella says. "Sounds from the shafts near our nest are growing louder. That must be a good sign. Mother Nature is looking out for us."

"To me, those whistling sounds are weird," Merlin grunts from behind.

When I reach Georgia's block, I peer down the road. Kids are arriving. No way I can roll right up with Gabriella and Merlin hovering beside me. So I ride on.

Sarafina nags, "You're going the wrong way. And who are you talking to?"

"The eagles. They're back."

"Birds? People can't talk to birds," she says. A second later, she adds, "Though, there was a case documented in 1804 of the native Māori people of New Zealand singing with whales."

"And Jane Goodall talks to gorillas!" I say, and rev the MagBoard. Around the corner, I tell the eagles, "You've gotta go now!"

"Fine, but we can't wait forever," Merlin squawks. He flexes his claws as though he's practicing for a brawl. The birds slow and fall behind. I race onward. But now I'm late.

Tied to the white iron gate, three red balloons bob toward the doorway. I glance back to be sure the coast is clear, then walk up the sloped pathway to the two-story mansion fit for a princess. But not Snow White, of course—more like Cinderella after she marries the prince. By the pillars, I take a deep breath. If I turn back now, I can still make it to the Safe Haven. But the music pumping on the other side of the door lures me in like the sirens of ancient Greek mythology.

I ring the bell.

"Welcome!" a woman's voice chimes. The door swings open. Before me is a grand entrance like in a fairy tale. Above hangs a chandelier—real crystal, of course. A marble staircase sweeps up and around. At the center of the foyer is a round table. Set upon it, a ginormous vase holds three dozen red roses. Their thorny stems stand guard, protecting each bloom that casts the sweetest smell of honey. I stand on my tippy toes to catch a whiff.

"Well, hello, our new star player. Nice to meet you, KyRose," Georgia's mother says. Her platinum blond hair—no longer tucked beneath a baseball cap, like at the games—spills over her shoulders. A taller, older version of her daughter, Mrs. Schmidt wears a poodle-white sweater studded with LED rhinestones. Surely, it's another of her own designs. "I've seen you play," she says. "You're good. Real good. I like that…and the way you pass the ball to my Georgie. Keep it up!"

Georgie? No one at school calls her that!

"They're all out back." Mrs. Schmidt motions the way, then sips from the purple nectar sloshing in a martini glass cupped between her red fingernails.

"Oh…hmm," I stutter, stunned. I'm like a deer caught in the headlights. I can't move…between the palace entrance, the blinking rhinestones, and now her *drinking* at a kids party.

"Oh, this?" She lifts her glass, noticing my stare. "It's just juice. Your dad's stuff. I'm a fan," she says, nudging me down the hall. In the huge living room are cozy, chic sofas huddled around low coffee tables. Floor-to-ceiling glass doors open onto a sprawling backyard with an Olympic-size pool. Floating in the pool are hundreds of balloons that glow, all red. Music is blasting and everyone is here. I even recognize a few FriendZ celebs, along with the usual suspects—Dante, Dillon, Avery, Rex, and Tabeen. Rebecca stands outside with the chorus crowd, huddled by the buffet. They eat chips dipped in a creamy orange goo. When she sees me, Rebecca breaks away and walks over.

"Isn't this awesome? You missed the jugglers, but you've gotta see the dance room." Rebecca pulls me into the darkened room with twinkling lights. There's a DJ and a CINE-A-Matics travel machine. Projected, spinning on the walls and up on the ceiling is…Paris.

"We're at the top of the Eiffel Tower. It's so jam!" I can't help but gush.

Rebecca tugs me onto the middle of the dance floor. Bodies groove, laughing, having the best time. There's Georgia with Dante. She waves me over as she peeks at her bracelet.

"Since you're late, I thought you might be bringing your brother. Is he here?" She cranes her head, looking around behind me.

Huh? She can't be serious? "Sorry, Jack couldn't come. He's busy," I say, but don't mention he's with his girlfriend. Dante shoots me a crooked look. Obviously jealous, he twirls Georgia around until she giggles. Avery and Dillon shake their hips to the beat. Rebecca and I dance too. The energy in the room is electric. A wind machine blows gusts of lavender. It's like true Paris. I'm on top of the world. We dance for what seems like hours. Scenes change with every song. We travel to Mt. Fuji in Japan and the Sydney Opera House in Australia. At times, we're flying and at other times, we're inside a castle. Chandelle Waterhouse's song plays as we wander through a forest with millions of monarch butterflies all around us. I think of Abuela and magic. A sweet sensation rushes through my veins. But then, Rex grooves up beside me, streaming a video. I turn away. I can't be caught on camera. Cora will see! I step outside.

"Having fun?" Georgia asks as we stand in the garden.

"Yeah! It's the best time ever! Thanks for inviting me."

"You're one of us now. A Prima and a key player. I can rely on you?"

"Sure. Always," I say.

"Monday, we play the Victorians again. Think you can handle it this time?" Her eyes shift to her mother, who brings out a tray with cut-up watermelon. The pieces of fruit are skewered on sticks and arranged in the shape of a huge heart. Her mother beams a smile at Georgia, and places the tray at center of the buffet. "We have to beat 'em!" Georgia says. She looks at me. "And go on to win the champion title. Got it?!" She purses her lips.

I shoot her a thumbs up and pray that Cora gets that vest back. Georgia sways her shoulders and hands me a cup of punch. It tastes of pineapple and coconut.

"And, oh." Georgia leans forward. "Those mantis shrimp goggles you made? I really like 'em. I can see lines on flower petals and a whole new world of color. It's cool. But I know you didn't do it alone."

I gasp, afraid she's mad at me.

"No, it's fine. It's actually smart, the way you used Will like that."

Used him? Is that what I did? My stomach pinches—though, it could be the acid from the pineapple. Georgia chuckles and takes another sip. "The problem I have now…isn't with you. It's with *her*." She points at Avery, who's sitting across the pool on the other side. "Can you believe it? She wants to change the goggles so the frames are purple and decorate 'em with freakin' polka dots!"

"Well, maybe…," I start to say.

"You're not picking her side, are you?"

"Of course not."

"Good." Georgia slips her fist under my elbow, so we're arm in arm. "Let's take a velfie!" She jiggles her new drone camera out of her pocket. She'll post it on FriendZ, I'm sure.

"Uh, let's take it later," I say. "I have to go to the

bathroom."

Georgia shrugs, then prances off toward the pool to hold court. I walk towards the buffet but Georgia calls out, "The bathroom's inside, down the hall to the left."

Halfway down the corridor, I come upon Georgia's mom's design studio. Inside are bins filled with LED diodes and different colored rhinestones. No one's coming, so I dip inside. Sketches of designs—shirts, sneakers, backpacks—are projected on the walls. I dig my hand into a pile of silver rhinestones. They glimmer like crown jewels and I imagine myself dressed glitzy head to toe. I hear a voice down the hall. Quickly, I shove a handful of rhinestones into my pocket and scurry out.

By the pool, I turn and can't believe it. There's Will!

"What are you doing here?" I ask. He's wearing skinny jeans and a sleek button-down shirt. "You clean up nice," I say.

He blushes and his dimples shine. "I could ask you the same question," he says. "Though, I had a sneaking suspicion I'd find you here."

"You didn't tell Cora did you?!"

"What? That I was coming here? She didn't ask. Nice party, huh?" He looks around. There's got to be at least a hundred kids here by now.

"Promise you won't tell Cora you saw me!"

"Don't worry. Your secrets are safe with me. I told

you that already. But be careful—when you lie to your friend, chances are, you're gonna get caught. You know that, right?" Will warns.

"I know what I'm doing!"

"Do you? Okay, boss!" He smiles half-heartedly. "So, you gonna ask me about Misty?" His eyes light up like stars.

"What happened?"

"Using our schematics, Troy built her a vest. Got the emitter right too. All waterproof. Misty freaked out when he strapped them on her. If you were there, you could have calmed her down. Anyway, she gave in after a while, and was wearing it when I left."

"Oh good! So we'll get *our* vest back?" I hold my breath.

"Yeah. Cora's got it."

I let out a sigh of relief. "Soooo, how did you get invited to the party, anyway?" I ask.

"Georgia. She said she wanted to 'thank me' for, you know, the goggles."

I squint, giving him a look.

"I promise I didn't tell her. You know she's got spies."

"Oh, I know!"

Avery laughs from across the pool next to the trampoline. On top of it Dante, Dillon, and Rex tumble around. Dante wrestles the boys and sits on top of them. He then spots me and Will, and makes his way over.

"Hey, squirt. What are you doing here?" Dante asks, poking Will in the shoulder. "Think you're clever, huh? Well, you're not. You're just a nerdy mama's boy."

Will's face turns white, then red.

"Dante, stop!" I shout. But he doesn't listen.

"I'll say whatever I want." Dante pokes Will harder. Will stumbles back. "Yeah, let's see how tough you are. Bet you're too scared to jump off the roof into the pool. Ha ha ha!" He keeps laughing, and so does the crowd that gathers around us.

"Sure! I'll do it!" Will says, taking the dare.

My heart lurches. "You could drown," I say. "And you hate water. You don't have to do this!"

"I'm not scared!" Will shouts it out loud so everyone can hear. He then climbs up the gutter and onto the roof. Music blares. The entire party moves outside.

Dante cackles, "Prove yourself, boy!"

Will beats his chest and grunts like a gorilla. A chill runs down my spine.

The crowd chants, "Do it! Do it!"

"No, *don't* do it!" I yell. But then I see Avery. She stares at me, clapping and chanting with the rest of them. Will steps to the edge of the roof. Rex pulls his camera out. Everyone does. Avery keeps staring at me. The crowd presses, and I too begin to chant, "Do it! Do it!"

Will leaps. I shut my eyes. Splash! I run and kneel beside the pool. Will wades over and I grab his collar. "You could have killed yourself!"

He nods faintly, clearly winded. Meanwhile, the crowd goes wild.

"Awesome!" Georgia stands over us. "I got the whole thing on video." Her drone flies around. Will climbs out of the pool. "Let's get a photo," Georgia says. "My followers will die for this!" she boasts. Will poses beside her. "KyRose, get in here," she says. "What? You don't want to be popular? Fine, suit yourself."

"No, wait!" I jump into the shot. *Snap!* Smile! *Snap!*

The crowd picks Will up onto their shoulders. We cheer on.

Georgia's mom comes outside. "What's going on?"

My bracelet begins to zing. Hearts and sprinkles flood my feed and my FriendZ requests soar to 976.

Definitely the best party ever! I relish the moment, and push Cora out of my mind.

Sixteen

Haywire

Monday morning, on the way to school, I'm in the car. I look out the window. No Gabriella or Merlin. Only a plane moves across the sky. The jet leaves a trail of two white lines. Abuela always complained that exhaust from jet engines poison our planet. Yet, in a matter of seconds, the lines break up and disappear as though they were never there. Maybe that'll be the case with Cora? She'll forget I ever lied to her.

As I walk across the front lawn of school, Skinner is nowhere in sight. I kneel by the knobby trunk of the jacaranda tree and hide a few nibbles of an oatmeal-sunflower biscuit.

"Hey, KyRose!" I spin around. It's Georgia. We hug. "You won't believe how many new followers I got from that video with Will. 1222!"

"Whoa! Me too. I got 1178. And more likes than I could ever imagine."

"You gotta keep posting stuff now," Georgia says, slipping her arm through mine. Together we walk up the steps. "Ready for the game? To show those Victorians who's boss?!"

"Bring 'em on," I say, then stumble on the step. Georgia catches me. I pray that Cora brought the vest!

In FabLab, Will and I sit at our table. Ah-choo! He sneezes.

"Are you sick?" I ask.

"I'm fine." Will blows his nose in a crumpled tissue that he pulls from his pocket.

Cora walks over and tosses our vest onto the table. I reach to snatch it.

"Not so fast!" She puts her hand over it.

"What's up?" I ask, backing up my chair.

"You tell me." Cora squints and waits. I had a whole apology ready to go…*I'm sorry, I didn't mean to lie. We can still be friends. Right?* But none of it spills out of my mouth. I just sit there and listen to Georgia's giggles as she replays the video from across the room.

Class starts. "Today, you'll go around the room, visiting each other's projects, and demo your gadgets," Mr. Bracket says.

"Ask questions and gather feedback, so you can improve your prototypes," Ms. A says. "Let's go!" She claps and Cora's gone...over to Miriam's table. But she leaves the vest behind.

"Didn't you talk to her yet?" Will leans over and whispers. "You know, to clear things up?"

"Well, I left her a message yesterday. And she didn't call me back. Best to forget about it," I say, glancing at Georgia's table.

"You sure about that?" Will asks.

"Yeah." I think about the lines of toxic fumes disappearing behind the airplane. "Look, she's already forgotten about it." I tip my head toward Cora, who's busy showing Miriam code on her tablet. I pretend the lie is gone, like it never happened.

"Come on." I grab the vest. Will and I head over to Tabeen's table. She wears a rainbow bodysuit spun from spider genes. "Bullet proof and fashionable," she says, twirling around. "Not boring like the clothes my parents are gonna make me wear. Once I turn thirteen, I'll have to wear dull-colored, long dresses with sleeves that reach to the moon. It's hard enough keeping this hijab stylish," she says, adjusting the pale yellow scarf wrapped around her head. She twirls around again, modelling the whole outfit. "Do you like it?"

"Ah-choo!" Will sneezes.

"Maybe I should add a heater to my bodysuit?"

Tabeen says, rubbing her arms. "Like Georgia's pool, Mars is very cold!" She winks at Will.

I then strap on our vest and walk around her table with my eyes closed.

"Awesome, but it could use a style upgrade for sure," she says. "Like if it were pink or yellow—something bright and cute. Oh, I know…what if we could plug your vest into my bodysuit, and astronauts could wear them together?"

"That's an idea." Will sniffles. "We'd just need to add a port…maybe here." He pokes me in the ribs.

"Ow!" I yelp.

"Oh, didn't you see that coming?" he jokes.

"No." I don't laugh. What if Troy *did* mess something up? I check the wires. Everything seems fine. At least, for now.

"Go Jaguars!" Mrs. Schmidt hollers from the stands, her rhinestone cap in place again. A few rows up are Rex, Dante, and Dillon with headsets on, ready to play *Smash Spectator*. Cora sits at the other end of the bench. I'm surprised but happy to see her. Maybe she'll root for me after all. Cora wears her silver-framed scopes, and on her lap is a black box with a short antenna sticking out of it.

Georgia taps me on the shoulder. "Ready!?" She runs out to the middle of the field with the ref and Marta.

The vest zings under my layers. When the coin falls to the ground, Marta cheers. Victorians get the ball first. The rest of us hustle onto the field. I stand guard by our goal while my teammates scatter to their positions. The ref blows the whistle and Marta kicks the ball to Tommy. Quickly, and skillfully, the two tag-team and cross mid-field into our territory. But this time, I sense their every move as I slip into *The Zone*. Time slows. My chest relaxes, my arms reach out. I know where to look, when to turn. It's my new instinct.

As striker, Georgia has to stay back, so it's up to Rebecca and Tabeen to pry the ball away. Marta kicks. The ball flies over Rebecca's head. I jump. The sensors light up and neurons fire. My hands hug the ball. "Got it!"

Georgia waves. I kick the ball to her. Her mom shoots me a thumbs up from the stands. Georgia then scores! We're up, 1-0.

Marta dribbles back, elbows out. As she nears—twenty feet away from me—I stay calm and ready. I even close my eyes. I see her cleats and the ball, but suddenly, my vision wanes. The nodes on my back go dead. When I open my eyes, it's too late. The ball has sailed into the net. Victorians cheer. Georgia throws her arms up, fuming. My palms, held hostage in my gloves, break out in a horrific sweat.

I slap my bracelet, taking it off sleep mode, then

fumble though my pocket for my earbuds. I slip them into my ears, hoping Coach Hartley doesn't see. "Sarafina, fix this!" I whisper in a panic. "Troy must have messed something up."

"Well, maybe you're better off!" she says, but I don't need a lecture.

"Not now!" I rail. Just then, the vest starts up again. I close my eyes. The sonar is back. I play like a fiend. We win the game 3-1. Mrs. Schmidt blows kisses from the bleachers. But Cora is gone.

Rex jogs over. "Hey, KyRose. Killer game! How about an interview?"

Georgia waves at me from across the field.

Rex nudges me. "Open stream. You and me." The beetle drone he rebuilt buzzes over our heads.

"Talk to our captain," I say, motioning toward Georgia, who's now running over toward us.

"With moves like that, it's you who should be captain, not her!" he says. "Listen." Rex spreads his arm toward the stands. People are chanting *my* name.

༄

Come Friday after school, I skip into the house. "Hey, Alfred. It's a glorious day, isn't it?" I smile.

"If you say so, Miss."

"Oh, come on. You're doing a great job." I swipe my finger across the entryway table. "See? No dust."

Alfred's eyes blink—blue lights flashing.

"Now that's the spirit!" I pat him on the back.

Puddles bounds down the stairs. "You're home! Did you win?"

"Of course, we did! Third game this week!" I scoop him up and give him a kiss.

My bracelet zings with a message from Georgia. *Want to go shopping and sleep over at my house tomorrow?* I fling back a thumbs up, even though I need to ask Mom and Dad first.

I catch a whiff of fresh ginger and head to the kitchen. Alfred bends to grab my duffle bag.

"Don't touch that!" I say. The last thing I need is him throwing my vest into the wash, ruining everything.

In the kitchen, I tell Dad about our winning streak.

"Excellente, mi amor!" He lifts me and spins around. "Now, can I *finally* come to your game to see you play?"

"Definitely. Mom too. Georgia and I are unstoppable. The whole school is rooting for us. Except, well…."

"Who? Who's not rooting for my girl?"

"Cora." I thought she'd come around by now, but she's still giving me the cold shoulder.

He pours me a ginger-apple juice with a squirt of aloe. It tickles my throat and tastes like truth serum.

"So? Want to tell me what's going on?" Dad shifts his weight side to side like a boxer.

"Well, you know Georgia," I say.

He nods. "Captain of your team."

"Yep!" I tell him how her mom's a big fan of his. Dad smiles. "Oh, and Georgia invited me for a sleepover tomorrow night. Can I go?"

"Sure," he says. "But go on."

I tell him how, now that Georgia and I are always together, "Cora is well…she's, she's…." My mind whirls.

"Jealous?"

"Huh. I never thought of it that way," I say, looking up at the ceiling.

"Well, you still want to be friends with her, right?" Dad asks.

"Uh, yeah."

"Show her your loyalty," Dad says.

"But how?"

"You'll think of something."

I will?

Seventeen

Journey Underwater

The next morning, Puddles jumps on my bed while Sarafina plays me a message just in from Troy. It's sent in a group chat to me, Will, and Cora.

"Hey, good news! Misty's vitals are up. She's eating, swimming." A video shows Misty racing round the tank, darting and diving. "According to the patterns in her movements," Troy goes on, "she's using sonar. The implant's working! But still no news on the whereabouts of her pod. Not yet, anyway. I'll keep you posted." The message ends.

I reply with a shooting star emoji. Will sends a thumbs up. Nothing from Cora.

What can I do to prove to her that we're still friends?

I get the urge to doodle because it helps me think. I pull open the top drawer of my desk to grab a pencil. Beside it is the yellow Post-it note I took from the Safe Haven.

Hey, that's it!

"Sarafina! Wake up."

I log in to the Safe Haven computer system using the password. GPS access is DENIED, but that's okay! I'm not after Gabriella. Bingo! On my dashboard are the ROVs, all twenty-five scattered around the islands.

"Sarafina, pull up this reef." I show her the snapshot I took of the holographic map with coordinates for latitude and longitude of where I thought I saw the cave.

"The reef is called Farnworth Bank," Sarafina says. "Located 1.6 miles off the coast of Catalina."

"Which ROV is closest to there?" I ask.

"The *KnifeFish*," she says.

"Good! Intercept and redirect it to Farnworth Bank. I'll be right back." I run into Jack's room. Luckily, he's already gone for the day—location scouting with Emily like they usually do on Saturday mornings. I rummage through his closet. Tucked in the back, behind two beat-up skateboards and a ski jacket, I find it. His old A/VR bodysuit used for gaming. It should fit. I sling it over my shoulder. It's heavier than I expect—made of neoprene with metal threads and 2,000 haptic sensors running through it, it's enough to make anything feel real.

I'm meeting Georgia in an hour to go shopping, so I work fast. From a rack on the wall, I grab the immersion gloves and Jack's new A/VR/HMD-822 headset. He got it for free from a sponsor, so he won't mind if I use it, right?

I run to my room and drop the accessories onto my bed, then go back and drag the Roto VR cockpit from his room into mine.

"Sarafina, activate headset and cockpit."

Will and I already added a port to the echolocation vest, thanks to Tabeen's idea. So the rest should be easy. I snap the USB-E cable into the vest, then stick the other end of the cable into Jack's old bodysuit.

"Sarafina, integrate systems," I say.

"Sure thing. But…what for?" she asks.

"An insurance policy! With sonar and a full immersion A-VR bodysuit, I'll have a better chance to see what's in that cave. When I find it, that is."

"The *KnifeFish* has sonar onboard," Sarafina says.

"Good, so I can emit sound waves from there. Just make sure that when the sound waves bounce, they go right into the vest," I say.

I then peel off my pajamas and toss them onto the dresser. They land, tipping over the kachina doll.

Quickly, I grab the bodysuit and step into one leg, then the other. My fingers dig into the rubbery neoprene. I stretch and pull it over my hips, then stick my arms in. *Zip.* I grit my teeth. Cinderella's slipper, it is not—more like the ugly stepsister! I can barely breathe. I guess I'll get used to it. Over the bodysuit, I strap on the echolocation vest.

"Sarafina, override autopilot."

"You sure? Aren't we breaking rules? This is a secured system."

"We're not breaking anything. I've got the password." I think about Cora snooping around the FriendZ archives without a care. She's probably looking through my posts right now. I need to make things right with her. If I can just find the cave, she'll know I still care about her and Misty. "We'll just take a quick spin," I say. "Now do it!"

I flip the seat down in the cockpit and release the joystick. I scoot in and buckle up the four-point harness seatbelt. I feel like an astronaut. Though their rides get bumpy, mine will be smooth. What could go wrong?

"Sarafina, power *on*."

"Are you sure about this?"

"Yes!"

The bodysuit comes alive. A tremor cascades over my shoulders, then down my arms and chest. It tickles my stomach and grips around my hips and thighs all the way to my ankles. I slip on the gloves, and they vibrate and squeeze around my fingers.

"A/VR suit is fully active," Sarafina says. "Overriding autonomous mode on the *KnifeFish*. Controls are in your hands. Cameras coming into view."

Inside the headset, my screen changes from static blue to black. "I can't see a thing."

"Your pupils are dilating," Sarafina says, reassuring me.

"Power on echolocation," I say. Nodes zing on my back, and I scan with sonar. But it's quiet. As my eyes adjust, blackness fades to aqua blue with swaying streaks of sunlight.

I twist the joystick to the right. The ROV turns and I tilt sideways. So real. I feel an upward push on my right side. That's centrifugal force, Sarafina explains. Has to do with gravity. Within minutes, I forget I'm in my bedroom. Instead, I'm exploring open waters like a real knifefish.

A map overlays my screen, and I begin the descent…twenty, thirty, forty feet deep. The top of the reef comes into view. It's blanketed with purple hydrocorals. Its Latin name, *Stylaster Californicus*, pops onto my screen. A parrot fish swims over and presses its lips onto the *KnifeFish*. I can feel it suckling on my arm. I continue down, passing shelves of reef, and swerving around razor-sharp pinnacles. A scorpion fish changes color, leering from a crevice. Tiny green eyes stare at me from slits and gaps. Hundreds of other fish hide in the pockets of rock. A jolt of excitement bursts inside me. Life everywhere, and I'm smack in the middle of it! At sixty feet down, a school of thirty mackerel shimmer around me. The ecosystem is rebuilding! I have to tell Gabriella and Merlin. But suddenly, the mackerel get spooked and dart off, as though something were chasing them. The further I descend, the narrower the path becomes. The last streaks of light disappear. Darkness all around me. My vest zings and I see a jellyfish swim along, shooting water through its stomach, with true jet propulsion.

"Twelve more feet and you'll reach the bottom." Sarafina says.

I inch slowly down the narrow crevice. Goosebumps prickle over my shoulders. Finally, the walls give way, and the passage widens as I reach the sandy bottom. I look around. There it is! Just like in my vision. I found it! The cave. I can't wait to tell Cora!

"How wide is the opening?" I ask Sarafina.

"The mouth of the cave is five-feet-and-seven-inches wide" Sarafina says.

I emit a sound wave into the cave. It bounces back. My vest tingles and I see a long corridor, twisting and turning. I catch a shape of something moving inside.

"Sarafina, I'm going in."

Cora will want to know what's inside.

"You'll barely fit."

"I've got to try." Gently, I lean on the joystick. The *KnifeFish* edges forward. First, the sound hits. Then, my neck snaps back with a force like Poseidon raging his trident sword. A tidal wave. I'm caught! Tumbling, I can't see which way is up. I squeeze the joystick with both hands.

"Steady! Come on, baby!" I shout. No response. I'm out of control, somersaulting like crazy inside the cockpit.

"Sarafina! Help! I can't breathe."

"The rudder's jammed. Turbulence is too great. We have to disengage." Her words come through choppy.

Nauseous. Dizzy. Spinning. "Quick! Do something!" I yell.

"The ROV's not responding. It won't let me disconnect," Sarafina says.

"Pull the plug! Eject! Get me out of here," I yell unable to catch my breath.

"I'll sever the circuits," she says calmly. "I'm programmed to keep you safe."

I hear a sizzle and smell burnt toast. My screen cuts out, going back to static blue. It worked, but my stomach is still spinning. My seat slowly stops, but I'm hanging upside down. I scoot my tush and swivel the seat right side up, then yank the headset off. Back in my room.

"What was *that*?" I ask Sarafina. I step out of the cockpit. My hands and knees are trembling.

"It was a current, like an undertow," Sarafina says. "But strange—undertows typically occur only near shallow shores, not in deep water like this. Searching oceanography databases now. Confirming, no natural force such as this has ever been reported. And, KyRose, the undertow was coming from the cave."

"I have to tell Cora. Will and Troy too." I unclip the vest. Under one of the nodes is a small rip. I reach for the sewing kit in my bottom desk drawer.

Just then, my digi-bracelet flashes. It's Georgia!

"Aren't you coming over? We were going shopping. My mom made appointments for us at the nail salon too."

"Yes. Sorry I'm late. I'll be right over," I say, and shove the vest into my JellyBag. I'll have to mend the tear later. Before I leave, I fling Cora a quick note. "Found the cave, and there's more to tell." I hit *send*, and hope it's enough to prove we're still friends.

But now, it's time to go shopping!

Eighteen

Caught in a Web

The rest of the weekend, I spend shopping with Georgia. We get matching electric tattoos and mani/pedis with animated candy-corn stripes. (After all, like Cora said, it's fall and Halloween is around the corner which means more parties. Yay!) Georgia posts on FriendZ everywhere we go, tagging me. I try on a bomber jacket and pair of pinstripe parachute pants—these are brand new, not like the pre-owned, thrift shop clothes I usually wear. Snap. "Totally jam. Buy 'em," Georgia says. So I do, along with a pair of Bone Bud earrings that I see in the glass case by the check out. They're ruby red studs. I pay, then slip the earrings through the holes in my earlobes. I got my ears pierced when I was little, so I barely remember the pain. I give the studs a pinch. They turn on. I then connect them via Bluetooth to my bracelet. Sarafina pops up the mirror app.

"Thanks," I say and check them out. They look exactly like earrings. No one will be able to tell the difference.

In the next boutique, Georgia stares at my sneakers. I try on black patent boots, like hers, and decide to buy them too. I hand the boots to a salesgirl to scan. She has one of those Think-Its installed in her head, a purple light blinking behind her ear. I wonder if Dad has seen…the zombies are out. "That'll be fifty-six LunaCoins," she says. I swipe my bracelet.

"Denied. Your account is thirteen coins short," the salesgirl says with a sour face.

"Oh, uh, just a minute." I turn away, "Hey, Sarafina, can you get Dad to transfer coins into my account, please?"

A second later, "Sorry, he's not available," Sarafina says. "But I can negotiate a loan and payment plan. It'll come out of your next week's allowance."

"Fine! Do it," I say. A minute later, the salesgirl hands me the boots in a bag. I switch them with my sneakers and wear them out. Georgia snaps another photo.

My bracelet zings with more friend requests. By Sunday night, I'm up to a whopping 1551 FriendZ friends. Even Jack notices and tags me in a post. It's a photo of us when we were toddlers playing at the beach.

As I get ready for bed, I work up the courage to ping Cora again. No answer. I've avoided her on FriendZ ever since Georgia's party but check it now and see that Cora's offline. So, I plop onto my bed and scroll instead through my FriendZ feed. I'm watching dance moves and velfies from girls and boys I've never met before—at least, not in person. But they want to be friends with me. Charlene from Tennessee, and Toya from Barcelona, and there's Theo from up the street. Two hours fly by. Still no word from Cora.

༄

The next day, I stroll into the FabLab with my shiny boots, wearing my new jacket and pants. Everyone checks me out, even Avery. I relish the moment. Rex—his hair a beaming yellow today—pretends to take a video. I smile and flash a pose.

"Alright, class, let's get started," Mr. Bracket says, twirling his laser pen like a baton in a marching band. "It's show & tell," he announces. "Let's see the changes you made to your gadgets with the feedback you got from classmates."

Will and Cora aren't here yet. Sitting at our table, I pull out the vest. We may have added the port, but I completely forgot to fix the plastic weave. My finger finds the hole, and my mind travels back to the

KnifeFish creeping down into the reef. Two chairs screech beside me. I jump and crumple the vest. Cora stares at me suspiciously as she sits down.

"Nice threads," Will says. I tighten my grip on the vest. He points at my bomber jacket. I relax. "Not sure it's your style, though," he adds.

Cora nods nonchalantly, as if she's barely listening.

I want to tell them that bomber jackets are all the rage, what all the FriendZ celebs are wearing, but Cora looks so uninterested. So instead, I clear my throat and tell them about the *KnifeFish* and the undertow spewing out of the cave. "I was stuck in the A/VR. Locked like a prisoner," I say.

"Is the vest alright?" Will pulls it out of my hands.

"It's fine." I grab it back.

"I can't believe you stole the password," Will says.

"I can," Cora adds, crossing her arms.

"Did you tell Troy?" Will asks.

"Not yet. He might get mad."

"He won't as long as you tell him the truth now." Will arches his brows and ticks his head toward Cora.

I get the hint. I turn to Cora. "I'm really sorry I lied to you about going to Georgia's party."

Cora shrugs.

Will lifts his eyebrows again, this time toward the Mantis Kicker table. Georgia is there, dipping the rims of the goggles into a bowl of red resin to cover the polka

173

dots. Avery huffs, watching her.

Will looks back at me. I take a deep breath and tell Cora the truth about the goggles, how I asked Will to make them so I could take the credit.

Cora spats, "Anything else you wanna confess?" Her eyes narrow and she stares at the vest in my arms.

"Uhhh, no," I stutter and grip it tight against my chest. With nothing more to say, I drop my gaze…and lose myself in the reflection of my shiny new boots.

That afternoon, Dad cheers me on from the bleachers. He looks around, smiling, as fans call my name. I hope he's proud of me. We win 5-0. Georgia and I high-five and pose for photos. Mom doesn't take any because she never made it to the game, but Dad and Mrs. Schmidt get chummy. I guess I should be happy, but it makes me uncomfortable. That night at dinner, I plead with Mom.

"Think of the animals at the shelter. They need a safe home," I say, passing the salt. "Just build your arena in their parking lot instead? It's always empty."

"Don't worry, honey. They'll find another building to move to…some place inland."

"But Troy needs to be by the marina…to help Misty." I tell her about the dolphin. "And that's not all," I tell her about all the weird stuff going on around Catalina. Of course, I don't mention stealing the ROV.

She cuts me off with a frown, shaking her head. "Did your eagle friends tell you all this?" Then she leans over and strokes my hair, but I pull away. Skirting a look at Dad, she urges him to say something more, but all he does is stare at Abuela's seeds up on the shelf.

Mom tries, in her own way, to make me feel better. "Troy will figure it all out," she says. "Though I get the feeling he *could* use some help. He was pretty disorganized and distracted at the permit office today. But honey, my hands are tied. I can't disagree with Mr. Sphinx and risk getting fired, you know that. Now let's close the subject once and for all!"

Mom's right. I back off. Still, a nagging feeling tugs at my gut. I need to see Troy and at least tell him about the cave.

༄

The next day, I visit the Safe Haven after school on my own. I first say hello to Mabel and rub her neck. She coos. Then in the Ocean Lab, I splash the water. Misty races over. Strapped around her is the emitter and vest. Her version of the vest has wires connecting to nodes, like mine, but uses tiny suction cups like an octopus to hold the nodes tight against her back as she swims.

"KyRose, you came to play with me!" Misty opens her mouth. Inside is a ball as big as a baseball, made of Lucite. Clear as glass, I can see right through it. On a tray beside the pool, are three more balls.

"Sure," I say. "These must be to help you train."

She nods with her snout, and I toss the balls in different directions across the pool. They plop, sink, and disappear. A monitor beside me beeps, showing the location for each ball, and tracks the time it takes for Misty to retrieve them. She returns with one, then the other, until she's brought them all.

"Wow, you're fast!" I remember reading how sound waves move faster in water than in air. "How does it feel to have echolocation again?" I ask. "Does it help you remember anything more?"

"Yes! How much I love to swim." Misty slaps her tail.

"What about the cave?" I tell her how I saw it.

"I don't remember a cave, but there was something in my mouth." She smacks her tongue. "I was hungry, but this wasn't food. It was sharp and smaller than these balls. It was dark. Glistening, buried in the sand. I remember picking it up."

"Then what happened?" I lean up against the edge of the pool.

"I was going to show…my mother and my pod, I guess. The next thing I remember, I was trapped in the nets," Misty says, suddenly sad again.

"Don't worry. We're going to find your pod and get you home," I say, even though I have no idea how. "Where's Troy? I need to tell him something."

Misty motions with her snout toward the dock. I

walk to the edge of the deck. Two steps down is the dock. Troy is operating a crane with a cable, hauling something clunky out of the water. The crane's motor roars loud, drowning out even the construction next door.

I cover my ears and shout, "Hey, Troy!"

He looks over.

"I need to tell you...I stole—I mean, borrowed...."

"I can't hear you," he mouths and points to his ear. When he finally shuts the motor off, he swings the clunky metal onto the dock. It's dented up all over, and two of its eight cameras are smashed. I read the name on the side. It says *KnifeFish*.

"Oh my gosh! What happened?" But my mind pieces it together before he can answer. It never occurred to me to check on the ROV after Sarafina severed the connection. I just walked away...went shopping. Meanwhile, the undertow must have crashed the ROV into the reef. I feel terrible.

"Must have been a storm," Troy says. "I found it drifting at the same spot where the Maiden Voyage caught Misty. Think it's a coincidence?"

No. If the *KnifeFish* drifted to the same spot, that means Misty could definitely have been at Farnsworth Bank reef. The natural current would have swept her further offshore, just like the *KnifeFish*. And that sharp thing she said she had in her mouth, she could have found it near, or even inside, the cave. But I can't tell Troy any of this, not with the *KnifeFish* banged up so badly. He'll be mad and won't let me come around anymore. I won't be able see Misty or Mabel.

"Yeah, must be a coincidence," I say. I feel like a fly caught in a web. My stomach hurts, but my mind keeps racing. Sarafina said that weird undertow wasn't natural. That means it could be man-made, or a new discovery. I swear I saw shadows inside that cave. Something weird for sure. I need to go back and explore it, but I dare not use the password again.

Troy unlocks the belly of the *KnifeFish*. From its guts spill plastic bits—a straw, a wad of fishing line, and tiny pieces of broken Styrofoam. He shakes his head. "Too much garbage in the ocean. Luckily, our ROVs can vacuum some of it up, and use super-enzymes to break down the plastic faster," he says.

"What's this?" I ask, picking up a black stone from the bundle of trash.

"Might be glass…part of a soda bottle or something," he says.

The stone is cold between my fingers, and under the sunlight, it sparkles like that rhinestone I took from Mrs. Schmidt's bundle.

"Think I could have it…for my collection?" I ask.

"Sure. But careful, I don't want you to get cut." He then asks, "So why did you come to the Safe Haven? It's always nice to see you, but did you have a question or something?"

I stare back at the *KnifeFish* with all its dents. My stomach aches. "Uhh, no. I just came to see Misty."

"Yeah, the vest is working out great! She's really adapted. Like you!" Troy says.

"Thanks," I say. "Now we just need to find her pod."

"Frankie's on it," Troy says.

In the meantime, Misty will have to live in captivity. But for how much longer is that going to be?

Nineteen

The Zone

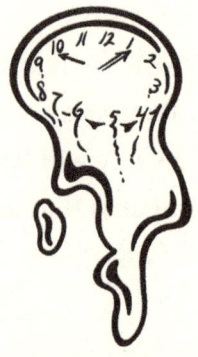

Coach Hartley has called a team meeting. We're in the locker room before practice. She sits on a stool and motions for our team to sit around her in a circle. "Congratulations, girls!" she says. "We're ranked number one going into the playoffs."

Everyone cheers.

"We've got an excellent chance to win the championship!" Coach says.

Rebecca and Tabeen high-five, and Georgia gives me a hug. Ordinarily, I'd flinch, but I'm not wearing the vest yet, so instead my head rises like a helium balloon. Meanwhile, Avery winces from across the circle. She and Georgia have barely talked since Georgia painted over her polka dots, and Avery hasn't sat with us at lunch all week.

Coach Hartley continues her pep talk. "Each of you needs to play your best, but as a team. That means being in sync with one another *and* passing the ball." She throws a look to Georgia. By now, we all know she's a hoarder.

"And, you, KyRose." Coach Hartley smiles at me. "You're definitely the most improved player." I sit proud. "Tell us, how do you do it? What's your secret?"

I gasp. My throat plunges to my stomach. Coach knows about the vest! That I'm cheating. The stool beneath her creeks.

Through my ruby red earrings that no can tell are earbuds, Sarafina whispers, "Biorhythms surging. Heart rate accelerated. You okay?" No, I'm not okay! The room grows dark. My head teeters. I feel like I'm about to faint.

"Go on," Coach Hartley leans in closer. All eyes are on me. I have to say something. My chest fills with air. A whiff of peppermint seeps in from the soap by the faucet. Then, a tingle flows through the circle. I feel the energy. I close my eyes and travel back to the soccer field…ball in the sky, nodes dancing, neurons firing, double vision sharp and clear. Everything is slow and I can hear the world around me, just like when I can hear animals.

"I slip into the *The Zone*," I say aloud.

"*The Zone*? What's that?" Rebecca asks, her lashes wide.

"Magic time," I say.

"What's that? Speak up," Avery demands.

"*The Zone* is like stepping into another world," I say. "Where time stops. I could be sketching or hiking," (I don't mention animals) "or playing soccer. I just get lost in *the moment*. It's like all the doors are open and I can go anywhere."

The stool creaks again as I hold my breath, waiting…for everyone to laugh.

"Exactly!" Coach Hartley exclaims. "Being an athlete is about focus and being in your body, yet also about being open and connected to your teammates."

"To *everything*, really," I whisper under my breath.

"That's why I'm assigning *you*," Coach says, looking straight at me, "to be co-captain of the team."

What? My heart lurches. I smile ear to ear, but when I look at Georgia, she looks miserable. Her lips pressed together like a road block, she stands up in a fury and marches off. A wave of heat and hate crashes over me. I shiver and think, that's just like her. Always competing. Always wanting to be *Prima #1*.

I stay seated. My teammates scoot over and fill the gap where Georgia was sitting, so the circle is complete again. They cheer my name. And, I love it!

Later at practice, as we run laps, Rebecca jogs up

next to me.

"Is it true? That stuff about *The Zone*? I mean, I've always felt like time stops when I'm, well…singing. Maybe I should…oh, forget it." She brushes her hand aside.

"What?"

"Try out for chorus?" Her eyes wander to the clouds.

"When you look up, the sky's the limit," I say.

Rebecca smiles.

Then Georgia hollers, "Faster, faster! We need to speed up to be champions!"

Rebecca drops her gaze and picks up the pace.

⁓

At our next game, the vest works fine. No interference of the signal or sound waves. Still, every ball I catch, I pass to Georgia. She scores three goals in a row. With two minutes left in the game, Rebecca waves. She's open. So is Georgia, but I kick to Rebecca this time. We're ahead, 3-0. Why not give someone else a chance? As Rebecca dribbles, I imagine she's singing to herself. She kicks and scores. We win the game 4-0, but Georgia sneers at me. She then snaps a velfie and a few photos of our team still on the field. When I look at my bracelet, her post already has 174 likes. But she's hasn't tagged me in it. My shoulders drop.

As I walk off the field, Rex runs up. His A/VR

headset is flipped up onto his purple spiked hair. He throws his beetle camera up into the air. It hovers between us.

"One interview? Your audience will love it! Mine too," he pleads, bent down on one knee.

I glance at my bracelet. "Sure, why not?"

In the locker room, I slip into a stall and change out of my vest like Superman, but I'm no hero. Sure, soccer is great, but I haven't saved anyone. Gabriella and Merlin are nowhere in sight, and Misty, well…she's still stuck in that aquarium. My muscles feel limp.

I head to Dad's Gut Love Juice shop down the street for refueling. Maybe he can cheer me up. Inside are five tables and a U-shaped counter. Blenders buzz, and the place smells like a spring morning after it rains. Dad brings me a Spirulina Mint Booster. On the monitor above the counter, an anchor woman reports news that the Think-It code has been *hacked*!

"Mira! I told you!" Dad says. "Now something really awful's gonna happen. Just wait and see." He then leans over the counter and asks, "So? How did things go with Cora?"

"Not bad, I guess, but she didn't come to my game today."

"Sorry I had to miss it too," Dad says. "But I see you played great!" He looks up through his scopes with a proud smile.

"You're not following me on FriendZ, are you?" I swat at the air in front of his scopes.

He holds the smile. "Wow, you're a professional. So talented." His eyes slide to the door. "Oh, here's your new best friend."

Georgia strides in with a digital e-reader rolled and tucked under her arm. "Hi, Mr. Sanchez," she says in the sweetest, highest-pitched voice I've ever heard her speak in.

"Hola. Nice to finally meet you," Dad says. "How about a Mint Booster on the house?"

"Sure, but add a shot of cayenne," she says, her eyes smoking. Her hair that's normally perfectly straight is scrunched and messy. When Dad walks off, Georgia throws the rolled reader in front of me. She then stands, hands on her hips. "So?" She huffs.

Slowly, I unravel the e-reader. The headline lights up in block letters. "Super Goalie Stops Everyone!" The video plays. It cuts from live-action shots of me blocking balls to clips from players on Smash Spector jiving with an avatar that looks just like me. It's even got the layers beneath my jersey. I've got to say, Rex did a brilliant job editing it.

"Didn't I tell you never, ever to give him an interview?" Georgia spews. "That's my job!"

"Uh, yeah, sorry," I say, and dare not remind her

we're now co-captains. I don't want to rile her up and cause a big storm. So instead, I slump my shoulders and eek out, "Won't happen again."

"It better not!" she turns and storms out of the shop.

Dad returns with her juice. "Where's Georgia?"

I tell him she had to go. "But I'll drink it," I say. With the coast clear, I look at the flurry of hearts and sprinkles on my bracelet, and accept *all* the friend requests coming in. When I'm done, my FriendZ friend total is at 6,572! More than even Georgia's got!

As I leave the juice shop, my mouth is on fire from the cayenne. I get a message from Troy. He says Cora, Will, and I need to come to the Safe Haven tomorrow. Could it be that he's found Misty's pod?

༄

In the lobby of the Safe Haven the next day, Will pulls Cora and me aside. He points his finger at us. "You two need to make up, once and for all. You're like revolving doors. Whenever one of you walks over, the other leaves. I can't take it anymore!"

Cora furls her brow. "Why would I be mad at *her*?" She looks at me with daggers in her eyes. It's like she knows I'm using the vest to cheat, but won't say it. And, I won't either! My chest pounds, but there's no way I'm giving up my FriendZ friends and all my fame. I have to keep playing soccer. It's the only way I can impress everyone!

"Come to the back," Troy interrupts through the intercom. Relieved, I slip ahead. Mabel squawks as we pass the rainforest. I'll have to see her on the way out. I pick up the pace, excited to hear Troy's news about Misty—maybe she's going home! As we step into the lab, my bracelet zings. It's an invitation to a Halloween party from a FriendZ celeb! I light up! But when I see Troy at his desk with a grim face, I get a pit in my stomach. Misty whistles, but I can't talk to her. Not until I find out what's going on.

"Bad news, I'm afraid." Troy says. He's got Frankie on the line. In the hologram, drenched in blue light, Frankie looks like he's in some sort of cockpit. Troy explains it's a submarine, and cuts to a wide-angle shot of the mini-sub that fits one person. I recognize the propeller from the pile of junk that Frankie had in his truck, the day of the field trip. The dents on the propeller are almost straight. The name on the side of the sub reads *Minnow Voyager*.

"Hey, kids," Frankie says. "Sorry, like I told Troy, after analyzing the data, there's still not enough mackerel. The ecosystem is only creeping back. Estimates project that Misty's pod won't be back until…." Frankie looks over his shoulder and jiggles something. It sounds like clinking glass. "At least a month, maybe two," he says.

"We have to wait that long?" Will says with dismay.

My heart sinks. Misty whistles again.

"Oh, and by the way, I found that cave. Nothing

there," Frankie adds, shifting in the cockpit.

"Did you go inside?" I ask, inching forward.

"Sure did. It was a breeze. I mean, a little tight with the sub. I had to angle in."

"Did you find anything at all?" Cora asks.

"Just rocks, water and a few crabs."

Cora and Will look at me and shake their heads disappointedly.

"Kids, there's something else that I need to tell you," Troy says, bobbing his leg.

"What's this? An eviction notice?" Cora picks up a pink slip of paper off his desk.

"That's just it! The city is kicking us out. We have to vacate immediately."

"So it is happening," Will says. "That explains the two bulldozers in your parking lot."

Bulldozers? I never even saw those on the car ride in…probably, because I was staring at my bracelet the whole time.

"I tried to convince the city," Troy says, "that the Safe Haven is better off here in the marina, rather than a gaming arena would be." He looks over at the fish and sea turtles swimming in the tanks. "But darn, those people at the Oyster Village are polished. They've got it together. They won."

A call comes in, Troy stretches his arms to get it, knocking the pile of papers off his desk. They scatter to the floor. Troy slaps his forehead, cussing under this breath. "No, not you," he says to the caller. "Yeah, I'll be right there." The call ends. "The bobcat is growling. Owls are hooting, hungry. I forgot to feed them all last night," he explains to us. "Oh, and the turtles are scratching too. I've got to clean their cages. I'll be back." Harried, he runs out.

While he's gone, Will says, "Boy, Troy can use some help around here. Especially now."

That's when Cora turns to me and says, "Wait! KyRose, doesn't your mom run *that* construction project next door?"

"She does?" Will's eyes grow as big as golf balls.

"Um, yeah," I say meekly. Will grunts at me.

Cora stomps her foot. "Well, talk to your mom! Make her stop!"

"I can't! I tried!" I clamor in defense of Mom—and myself. "I'm sorry!"

Troy returns, out of breath.

"It's not fair!" Will scoffs. "What's gonna happen to Misty?"

"I've made arrangements," Troy says. "She's going to live at Ocean World. The transport comes on Monday."

"But it won't be permanent, right?" Will pleads.

"I'm afraid it will," Troy says sadly. "With us having to move the Safe Haven, I just can't spend more time on trying to find her pod. Don't worry, she'll make friends with the other dolphins there who live in captivity."

"Sounds nice," I say. My bracelet vibrates. It's another FriendZ request. I tap *accept*. Jam. A tingle runs up my spine. I smile.

But Will snaps, jarring me. "It's *not* nice!"

"At least she'll be safe," Troy says.

I nod eagerly. Plus now, I can play soccer, be co-captain, and hang out with my friends on FriendZ, instead of worrying about dolphins and a creepy cave. Like Mom says, it's time for me to grow up.

"But Misty will be brokenhearted without her mother," Will says. He walks over and strokes her cheek. I stand back until Misty calls me over.

"KyRose, what's going on?" She slaps her tail. "Am I getting out of here?"

"Yes," I say, and force a smile. But I don't tell her the truth…that she'll never be free again.

Misty jumps into the air. Then suddenly, everything in the room stops. My hands grow cold and then my heart. I feel the blood seeping out of my chest.

Misty swims back and tips her snout, clicking and whistling. But no words. That's strange. On my way out, I stop in to see Mabel. I rub her neck. She doesn't say a word either. Not even a coo. As I pass the reptiles—bearded dragons, geckos, vipers—they're all silent. Even the wounded armadillo won't talk to me. All of a sudden, growing up seems very lonely.

Twenty

Epic Crash'n Burn

That night, I lie in bed trying to fall asleep. I hear Puddles snoring in Jack's room. Like Misty and Mabel, Puddles hasn't spoken to me either. He only barked when I got home.

Alfred pops his head in. "Go away," I yell. He flinches. His eyes flash, and he staggers off. Somehow, it's easier being rude to a robot than to my mother. I know Cora blames me for Mom's stupid boss pushing her to kick Troy out. But he'll find someplace to move the animals. Misty will be fine, I tell myself. Once she gets settled in at Ocean World, I'll visit her. Still, I can't sleep.

Sarafina rolls down the shades. Moonlight seeps in through the edges of my window. After we win tomorrow's game, the title will be within our reach. Just two more games after that. If I tread carefully, Georgia and I can share the fame. Still, I feel the weight of one hundred bricks across my chest. I've stolen Misty's hope. And what about Gabriella and Merlin? Maybe they fled, and I failed them too. Staring at the ceiling, my vision blurs, eyelids heavy.

Next thing I know, I'm hiking up a hill. The air is brisk, and the grass beneath my bare feet is cold. Over the ridge, I see Gabriella. My heart lifts. I call to her, but she doesn't hear me. I wave my arms. She circles, wings wide, hunting the ground below. Merlin swoops in. I wave frantically. My digi-bracelet dangles around my wrist, static shrieking from it. I flip it around. What?! The camera is live streaming. I yank and cover it. In that moment, the eagles dive toward me. But when they near, they don't slow. I duck, and their talons tear at my hair.

"It's me, KyRose," I cry out.

They squawk.

My heart clenches. "Talk to me!" I yell.

Not a word. I only hear the thunderous flapping of their wings. The eagles circle and plunge again.

I run. My feet tangle. I fall and roll down the side of the hill. The eagles follow, like torpedoes locked on target. I wrap my arms around my head. They peck at my elbows and stab my ribs. I scream.

Awake, heaving, I sit up in my bed and start to sob. Puddles runs in and jumps up next to me. He licks my face. Between gulps for air, I tell him about the birds attacking. But he doesn't say a word.

In a sliver of moonlight, I see the kachina doll laying fallen over on its side.

"Just a dream," Sarafina says.

In the morning, I jump on a MagBoard and take a detour.

"Where are you headed?" Sarafina asks. "School is the other way."

"I'm going to the Safe Haven. I have to see to Troy." A chill runs down my spine. I shiver and rub my elbows to be sure they're not eaten and bloodied.

"School starts in twelve minutes. You'll be late."

"I'll only miss homeroom and maybe first period. That's all."

"If you skip school, I'll have to tell your mom," Sarafina says.

"No, please don't."

"Sorry, I'm programmed to report your whereabouts and keep you on time," she says.

Argh! I'm done having a keeper, and that Australian accent of hers is starting to drive me crazy. Maybe I should shut Sarafina off? So what if I hurt her feelings? That setting is down low anyway. But, it's too late.

193

Sarafina runs on the cloud, so she's anywhere, anytime twenty-four hours a day, seven days a week. Her protocol and the algorithms she runs through will keep track of me using the MagBoard's GPS. I could switch boards to hide my tracks, but forget it.

"Fine!" I say and swerve back toward school.

∽

In the hall of trophies, I stare at the shiny statues. A championship trophy will soon be ours, and I'll be a star. Well, as long as Rex keeps streaming, that is, and I keep everyone believing I'm the greatest athlete alive. Way better than talking to animals like a freak, right? When soccer season ends, I'll play volleyball. Then in the spring, I'll join the track team. I'll jump hurdles higher and faster than anyone—the vest could help me do that, and if it doesn't, I'll deploy a hybrid and put spring-loaded coils in my shoes like the Mantis Kicker or find some other animal superpower to mimic. The possibilities are endless.

In the hallway, a bumblebee zips by. I think it's the same one I saw a few weeks ago, back when I was a nobody.

I bend over and ask, "Remember me?"

The bee doesn't answer.

I whisper, "You'll be cheering for me, right?"

The bee flies off. My mouth grows dry. I shake my head and once again, I notice the old plaque in the trophy case meant for science fairs and hackathons. Awarded to *Francis Maloney*. Hmm? Could Francis be *Frankie*? Troy did call his dad Captain *Maloney*. And, of course, Frankie said he went to school here. I stare at the plaque. *Electromagnetic field generator*, hmm?

"Whatcha doing?" A voice startles me. I spin around. It's Cora. She's wearing a rumpled sweater and has dark circles under her eyes. I'm about to show her the plaque, but then I see what's she's holding in her hands. I panic. I was just on my way to the FabLab to grab the vest. What's she doing with it? "I worked on it all night," she says, holding it up. "I added a new chip that has cellular coverage."

"Huh? Why do we need cell coverage?" I ask.

"Well, if it works, I want to add it to Misty's vest. You know, so I can keep tabs on her at Ocean World. I want to be sure she's okay. Don't you?"

"Yeah, of course," I say. "But the sonar? It's working just the same, right? You beta-tested it?"

"No. That's your job, remember? You can do it tonight." She hands me the vest.

"Can't we do it now?" I need to make sure the sonar is up to snuff before today's game. "It'll just take a sec," I plead.

"Sorry. Gotta go!" Cora smirks and walks off.

Quickly, I'm looking around for a place to test out the vest when Avery walks by. I shove the vest into my bag. A moment later, Georgia, Tabeen, and Rebecca skip up beside me.

"Game time," Rebecca sings with a jingle.

"Save it for the shower!" Georgia says, and rolls her eyes, then points at me. "Remember! No interviews."

I nod.

All the way to the locker room, we cheer "Jaguars #1" as I cradle my bag. Tapping my finger on the bulge, I pray the vest works, no glitches.

Huddled at the sidelines with Coach Hartley and the team, I look up at the stands. It feels like the coliseum in Ancient Greece—packed with fans. Georgia's mom sits up front, spine tall like a cobra beneath her studded cap. Georgia sneaks her a thumbs up. The game is about to begin. At the other end of the bleachers sits Dad, and Mom too. They wave at me. I adjust my headband and tug at my jersey. The vest vibrates beneath my layers. Double vision seems to be working fine, so far. I wave back at my parents and try to smile and relax.

Also in the stands are Jack and Emily, who holds her camera. The two of them whistle and cheer me on. A few rows up, Cora and Will sidle in and take a seat. Cora holds that black box again on her lap like she did at the last game that she came to. At the top of the bleachers, sits Rex, Dante, and Dillon. Rex angles his camera at the field, already streaming. I know because my bracelet zings with hearts and more FriendZ requests. Dante and Dillon put on their A/VR headsets. A group of thirty kids sit around them, all revved up to play *Smash Spectator*.

"Remember, girls! Keep your heads in the game—and stay in the *The Zone*." Coach Hartley winks at me. "Work as a team and pass the ball. Now go!"

Georgia punches the air. I pinch my earrings to make sure they're on in case I need Sarafina for anything. I swallow hard and run out onto the field. Our opponents, the Panthers, file in from the other end. *Panthers vs Jaguars*—two cats up against each other, fans stomp their feet. As I reach the goal box, a guttural squawk rattles my ears. I scan the trees. Vest tingling, I see thrashing in the canopy. I shudder and hug my elbows. With fear and joy, I search for Gabriella and Merlin. Perhaps, maybe, they still have faith in me…and I can help them somehow. But I see it's a family of ravens hopping along the branches. No eagles in sight.

The sun dips low and the whistle blows, snapping me out of my trance. Georgia elbows her way through players, ball at her feet. She scores. Everyone cheers. Panthers have the ball now. I hunker down. They kick. I jump, block, and kick the ball to Georgia.

Coach Hartley yells from the sidelines, "Pass the

ball," but Georgia hoards it and scores again. Rebecca looks over at me confused, half-cheering, half-disheartened. I feel bad, but can I take the risk? We have to win, and I need to keep peace with Georgia. So I ignore Rebecca, and each time I get the ball, even though she's open, I aim instead to my co-captain.

At half-time, we're up 3-0.

"We've got this, no problem. Just keep passing the ball to me," Georgia says, and lands me a high-five.

In the bleachers, Cora fiddles with the black box. From the top of it, she pulls the antenna and telescopes toward the sky. Then suddenly, the nodes on my back go silent. Cora knocks Will to get his attention, and the two of them point at *me*.

"Sarafina!" I rumble under my breath, then screech, "Kill the cell connection." Of course! It's Cora. She's jamming the signal. Taking revenge. I pushed her too far. Lied too many times. Disoriented and dizzy, I wobble. Behind a wall of shins and cleats, a Panther with pigtails kicks the ball. I lift my hands and jump. Soaring in slow motion, for a split second I think, *I can do this without the vest*. But then I blink, and fall to the ground. The ball swirls into our net. Georgia roars. I blink harder, pushing back the nausea swelling up. Then, suddenly, the nodes grow warm again.

"Cell is off," Sarafina says, and the vest is working.

I stand up, determined, but then Sarafina says,

"Wait, there's interference again!" I slash at my neck with my fingernails, signaling for Cora to turn the vest back on! She does. The nodes grow warm, then hot. I feel a tear and smell plastic burning.

Someone shouts, "Smoke!"

I feel the vest sliding down from under my layers. I tug it back up, but it falls again.

Commotion in the stands. Someone shouts, "Get a fire extinguisher!"

The girl in pigtails points. "What is that?" she calls out to her teammates.

Coach Hartley sprints over. "Are you okay?" Then, "Wait! What's this?" Her mouth hangs open.

Rebecca and Tabeen run up, eyes wide. Tabeen gasps, "KyRose? You're wearing your Echo Catcher…to play soccer?"

"I knew it!" Avery sneers. "You are a *cheater*!" She points a finger to my chest. It cuts through me like a laser beam. I can't breathe and slump over.

The ref blows his whistle in spurts. It pounds like a judge's gavel. As he stomps over, his sneakers crunch the nylon blades of grass and crackle like thunder under his footsteps. My legs give way. I collapse to the ground, my headband askew. Girls from both teams huddle around me, but not too close, less they touch the leper. Rex's drone dips low. I swat at it, as *Smash Spectators* boo and howl from the stands.

Georgia breaks through the crowd and stands over me. "See, I told you she was a liar," Avery hisses.

Coach Hartley shakes her head. I failed her and the team. "KyRose, we thought you had talent," she says, then looks over at the ref who blows his whistle once more and calls out, "Game over. Jaguars forfeit!"

"What a fraud. I can't believe I trusted you!" Georgia glares at me.

Desperately, I want to tell her, I cheated for us. But that's not true. I did it for me—so Georgia would take me under her wing and protect me forever, and so I'd be popular just like her. "I'm sorry," is all I can whisper. Ruined…forever. I want to die, and the ravens squawking up in the tree seem to seal my fate.

Later, as I leave the locker room, Mom and Dad are waiting for me in the dimly lit hallway. My heart sinks further. Oh, how I've disappointed them. Tears well up in my eyes. Georgia watches as we leave. I look back, searching for a glimmer of compassion in her eyes. Her gaze lifts to a quote on the wall. She tips her head and a glint stirs in her eyes as she reads it:

> *"The road to bold is paved with failure."*
> *— Peter Diamandis*

That's right. What an epic fail. I pull my hoodie over my head and disappear into the shadows of my parent's footsteps.

Twenty-One
End of a Hoax

That evening, sitting on the edge of my bed, I think of Ms. A and Mr. Bracket. They must be so mad and disappointed in me. Coach Hartley must've told them by now. She said she'd submit a full report to the principal's office too. I'll probably get expelled. The whole school—the whole world—knows I'm a fraud. Rex streamed it all—the vest smoking, the horror on my face. The video plays in a continuous loop, gone viral like a disease. There's a *meme* circulating on FriendZ—a picture of my avatar gone up in flames with the caption, "Liar, liar, vest on fire."

My bracelet has been zinging nonstop. I can't bear it. Still, I flip my wrist up and take a peek...maybe it's Georgia? Or Cora? But no, only another hater tagging me with an emoji that splatters egg on my face. What happened to the filtering agents that are supposed to block bullying online? I guess, as always, I'm the exception. I rip off my bracelet and throw it across the room. My life is over. No one *likes* me. Especially Cora. I know that now.

"She sabotaged me on purpose. Didn't she, Sarafina?" I ask, keeling onto my bed.

"Well, if you're talking about Cora, it's highly probable she was just testing the cellular coverage to be sure it worked."

"Oh, it worked alright! But she didn't say anything about operating it remotely *while* I was in the game. That must have been her last week, too, messing around, interrupting the connection. Of course! That's how she knew I was lying."

"Maybe it was emotional and her feelings were hurt," Sarafina says.

"Of course she was hurt!" I blurt.

"Humans are statistically prone to take vengeance when they feel they've been wronged. It's not what I'd call a positive trait, but then again, I'm not programmed to judge. Maybe if you had told her the truth?"

"Shut up!" I cut her off.

"Emotional. High blood pressure. Perhaps you should rest."

"Stop talking like my mother!"

"A-hem!" Mom clears her throat from the doorway. "I think you and that Amigo A.I. of yours have caused enough trouble. Don't you think?" Through her scopes, Mom taps and swipes her finger. The lights go off in my room, and with it, Sarafina.

"Come on. Downstairs. We need to talk."

In the living room where all our serious family meetings take place, Mom and Dad stand by the fireplace.

Alfred trots in. "Tea, ma'am?"

"Not now, Alfred," Mom says, and turns to me. "Breaking school rules, cheating. KyRose, that's not like you. What happened?"

"I failed. That's what!" I cross my arms, fuming. "And no thanks to you." My eyes narrow. "If you hadn't stolen Troy's permits, this would never have happened. There'd be no rush to free Misty. She wouldn't be going to Ocean World, and Cora wouldn't have revved up the vest in a mad dash. It would never have gone haywire and blown up like that." I know I'm ranting and talking nonsense, looking for someone to blame.

Puddles tiptoes over. Standing on his hind legs, he licks my thigh. I push him away with my knee. He whimpers and crawls under the sofa. Now I feel even worse. I'm such a loser. I throw myself onto the sofa and bury my face in the itchy wool tweed. If only I were a bug, or smaller still, a microbe, I could hide here forever, deep in the weave. I'd never come out, except for a drink of water or something.

"What did you say it was? Echolocation?" Dad asks in a gentle tone. "For your class project, right? To save animals?"

"No," I blurt, my voice muffled in the pillow. "It's to help the astronauts on Mars."

"And, for Misty?" Mom adds.

"Yes, for her too! But now," I punch the cushion with my fist, frustrated. "Everything's lost. Everyone hates me."

Dad sits on the edge of sofa beside me.

"Your invention is truly amazing," he says in a voice filled with kindness. I lift my head. He goes on. "I don't remember making sonar wearables when I was a kid. Mi amor, you love animals. Of course, you want to help them."

"No, I don't! They make me different and weird. I hate them."

Puddles whines under the sofa.

Mom kneels beside me. "Oh, KyRose. This is all my fault. Oh, my precious, love. I'm so sorry. I should never have told you to forget about what you love most." She strokes my hair. I start to cry, sobbing so hard my chest heaves. Tears stream from my eyes as I let it out—the fear of rejection, my hopes of being popular, the pain I feel inside from lying to Cora and Will, and pushing Misty away. I let it flow and it gushes out like a river.

Dad rubs my back. He says, "Abuela always told me to look within for the love I seek. I forgot that." He sighs, then blows Mom a kiss. I sit up. Dad thumps his heart with his fist and says to me, "Mi amor, I have faith in you." He wraps his arms around me. Mom hugs us too, and we hold each other for a long, long while.

With no tears left, I feel somehow younger, like when Mom and Dad used to hold me by my hands and swing me up into the air. Yet I feel older too. The living room glows with moonlight streaming in from the window. I feel lighter in weight, like a snake who's shed her skin to remove parasites. I'm more me, and for the moment, I feel safe. But I know the world out there still hates me.

Puddles pokes his head out from under the sofa and licks my ankles. I can't help but giggle. He jumps onto my lap and I hug him tight. I wish Abuela could be here too. She always made me feel safe, even when I knew I was different.

Twenty-two
True Colors

The next morning, I wake up. No alarm, no Sarafina. I sit up in a panic. "I'm late."

"You're not going to school," Mom says. "The principal called."

"So I'm expelled?"

"Suspended, just for a day. Not the whole rest of the year, luckily." Mom arches her eyebrows. "The principal said you should take today and the weekend to think about, well…what you've done." Mom pulls up the shades, then picks up my soccer jersey and shorts off the floor. She throws them in the hamper, and I wonder if I'll ever wear them again. I bet I'll be kicked off the team for sure.

"Hey," Mom says gently. "I took the day off work."

"You did?" I blink. Mom never misses work.

"We'll pretend it's Sunday. I'll take you to brunch. After, we can walk on the beach. You'd like that, right?" Mom picks up the kachina doll that's still tipped over on the dresser. She holds it for a moment, then carefully sets it upright. Then she turns. "Before we go," she says, "there's something I want to show you."

I follow Mom through the backyard and up the stairs that lead to Abuela's apartment. The wooden door opens easily, even though no one's been up here in months. The room smells of dry herbs. Gauzy curtains let in a pale light. In the corner, beside the window, is a painter's easel. An unfinished canvas of lush green palms sits on the floor, leaned up against two of the easel's tripod legs. In the room, there's also a bed, cabinet, loveseat, and a small kitchenette. Beside the sink is a tidy stack of dishes and Abuela's favorite teacup. The one I got her that says, "Grandmas give the best hugs."

Oh, I miss her so much my chest hurts.

From the cabinet, Mom pulls out a box of old photos. As we rummage through them, I come across a Polaroid of a young boy. He looks about six or seven years old and wears cropped pants and a striped shirt.

"That's your father," Mom says. He looks like Abuela…and me too. Big brown eyes and a wide forehead.

Mom pulls out another photo. It's of a woman, blond with green eyes who looks more like her. On the woman's lap is a little girl leaning over to blow out the candles on a birthday cake. "Is that you?" I ask.

"Yes. That was my fifth birthday." Mom bows her head. I inch closer on the loveseat. As tenderly as I can, I ask her to tell me more about my maternal grandmother.

"She always smelled of lavender when she hugged me. She grew up in France, in the countryside. Then, moved here before I was born. We always had lavender growing in our garden. I guess it reminded her of home. In this photo, she was already sick…with breast cancer." Mom sighs. "She didn't choose to die, but I blamed her for leaving me. I felt so alone. I knew, from then on, that I had to take care of myself. No matter what." Tears roll down her cheeks. I wipe them away. Her eyes are filled with love and sadness at the same time. Then her cheeks turn up with a smile. "Oh, and my mother loved to cook," Mom says. "Probably the reason I fell in love with your dad. Not just for his scrumptious enchiladas and juice." She laughs, tossing her head back. "But because of his passion. Your dad was quite a renegade when we first met. He used to protest against the sugar industry and try to save the Amazon from being cut down and turned into cattle ranches. You know how cow poo has all that methane that contributes to global warming."

"Gee, I didn't know that about Dad. That's why he gave me that book by Rachel Carson, huh?" I ask.

"Yes. He wants you to have a voice in the world," Mom says. She pulls another photo from the box. It's of Abuela wearing a floral dress, holding a parasol. Palm trees sway in the background. "Your abuela took me under her wing, like she did you. She said you were a seed, sprouting. I guess we all are, and we keep growing. I miss Abuela as much as my own mother."

Mom and I hug. I close my eyes and try to heal the little girl inside her, and in me too. We hold so tight, as if we could heal the world. And I think of Will, who doesn't have a mom anymore.

After Mom tucks the photos away, I ask her something I've been afraid to ask for months. Afraid to know the truth.

"Is Abuela ever coming back?"

Mom closes her eyes sadly. She shakes her head no.

My heart curls. I lose my balance and grab on to the edge of the loveseat. Tears well in my eyes. Mom puts her hands on my shoulders. As I stumble out of the apartment, she steps back in and pulls a drawer open from the cabinet. I see her slip something into her pocket.

When we get to the beach, Mom and I take off our shoes. I step off the cold cement onto the warm, uneven sand. Salt air rushes into my lungs. It's fresh, but stings my throat.

Mom walks us toward the dunes. Ten feet high, they run parallel to the shore. As we climb to the top, the crashing waves grow louder. We sit, gazing out onto the ocean. After a few minutes, Mom pulls out a small box. It has a purple ribbon tied around it in a bow, and with it is an envelope, its edges yellowed. Across it, written in cursive, is my name. It's Abuela's handwriting.

"She left this for you. Meant for you to have it on your thirteenth birthday."

"But that's still three months away."

"Yes, but I thought it could cheer you up. And given everything that's going on at school, Dad thinks too it might explain things. Mom tucks a strand of my fallen hair behind my ear.

I pull on the bow and open the box.

"Oh, it's beautiful." I hold up the gold chain. The charm hanging from it sparkles in the sunlight. It's a pair of wings stretched wide. Mom helps me put it around my neck. I rub the wings between my fingers and feel a tingle in my chest. Then, with trembling hands, I break the seal on the envelope. Mom reads it with me.

Dear KyRose,

This necklace is a symbol. A reminder that you are ready to fly. I wish I were there, in body, to hug you and to celebrate. But know, that I see you from the clouds, through the wind, through the eyes of a bird, and the scent of the sea. I am at one with nature like you, even in this form...as stardust.

KyRose, we come from the bloodline of the Equilibrar natives who strive to live in balance with the forest. Our people believe that long ago, we spoke the language of the animals and could communicate with trees and plants of all species. Yet over the years—centuries and millennia—we have lost touch. We've grown away from our brothers and sisters—the plants and animals—and forgotten that we are all part of nature. We must take care of the earth for future generations.

We humans have become arrogant, thinking we are better and stronger than the animals because we can build smart machines that give us the illusion that we can control nature. Don't be fooled. Nature is deep and wide and has sight into a greater world with multiple dimensions. Humans are limited by their five senses. They can't see all these dimensions. But animals and plants can show us the way.

Humans, at first, might doubt and belittle what they don't understand. Or they may call it "magic," but only because science hasn't yet been able to explain it. KyRose, mi nieta, trust in the mystery of the unknown. Bravely step forward. Only by reaching out and helping one another, and by remaining open to the sounds and spirits of nature, can we truly grow strong and be fully alive. Trust your connection to all of life so you may embrace your truth, my dear.

KyRose, you have a special gift. A power handed down to you from our ancestors—to tap into the intelligence of animals, to hear them, to speak to them, and to share their wisdom with the world. I saw the power when you were born, when the ravens landed on our roof the night you came home from the hospital.

Look inward and you will always feel your power, mi nieta.

People might make fun of you because they misunderstand you. You might lose your way, yet know that I am always with you. Fly...and wish and ask for what you need. Call to the butterflies, the ravens, and all who live in the sea. The spirit of your ancestors and I—and all of nature, and all of the universe—will answer your call.

Con todo mi amor,

Abuela

Mom's eyes swell up with tears. "I was trying to protect you. I didn't want you to be alone. I knew kids would make fun of you for being different. I wanted you to grow up so you could take care of yourself…like I thought I had to. But now I know, you'll always belong…to the animals."

"Mom, I'll always belong to you too. We're a family," I say.

She hugs me. "I love you so much."

Then her phone rings. She slips on her scopes. "It's Mr. Sphinx," she whispers to me. "I need to take it." She squeezes my arm, slow and gentle, nothing like the pinch she gave me in the car the day I forgot my duffle bag—when her real world never included talking to animals.

While Mom's on the call, I slide down the dune and head to the shore. Rubbing the charm between my fingers, I wonder aloud, "I wish I could talk to the animals again." From the corner of my eye, I spot a tiny pink claw jutting from a hole in the sand. It's a hermit crab. Its gray torso is stashed inside a coiled shell that's speckled beige, the same color as the sand around my feet.

"Get out of my way!" the crab shouts, scurrying sideways like crabs do.

"Wait! I can hear you!"

"So then skedaddle! Out of the way!" The crab raises

a claw.

I jump back to avoid its pinch, while my heart bubbles. I can hear what he's saying!

"Why are you just standing there?" The crab probes. "Are you going to make a hole and hide like me?"

"Hide? I'd need a much bigger hole than you," I say. My mind races to all the posts about me on FriendZ, and having to face everyone at school on Monday. I can't live in a hole forever. I have to venture out, even if I'm scared to death. Which I am!

This reminds of something Abuela told me and Jack. Mother sea turtles bury their eggs in the sand. After thirty days, the babies hatch and have to dig their way to the surface, then make a run for the sea. Their mothers are long gone, and the hatchlings have to swim and find their own way. But sea turtles, like Mr. Bracket said, can sense the Earth's magnetic field and use it to navigate their way. That's how, years later, they can find their way back to the same beach where they were born.

What about me? How will I navigate?

That's when I hear my name being called from the sky. "KyRose! There she is!"

I look up. "Gabriella and Merlin! You're back!" I shout, my heart pumping. The eagles swoosh low. The crab runs for cover, into its hole. I spread my arms out wide and the eagles land on my forearms. I hold them easily….my muscles have grown strong from soccer.

"Where have you been?" I ask.

"We brought someone." Gabriella tips her beak toward the ocean. Beyond the breaking waves, a spray of water shoots ten feet high. A silver fin looms and a dolphin bobs its head across the surface.

"*Click*, ahoy! You're the girl who speaks with animals! I remember you. From summer…surfing with your dad. I was with my pod. Remember? I'm Ollie."

I wade knee-deep into the water and see the speckled marks around his spout. "Yes, yes! I remember you, and that somersault."

"I need to find my cousin Nai'a," Ollie says urgently.

"Cousin?"

"It's Misty!" Gabriella says. "Nai'a's her real name."

"The eagles said she was alive. Is it true?" Ollie asks. I tell him she is.

"Can you bring me to her?" Ollie slaps his tail.

My chest pounds. I rub the wings on my necklace. *Only by helping one another…. A special gift….* Abuela's words echo in my head.

"Yes! Follow me!"

Twenty-three

Reunions

At the beach, I explain to Mom why I have to go. She waves at the eagles and to Ollie, and blows me a kiss. I then lead the animals along the shore toward the marina. We shortcut through the canals. That's when we almost lose Merlin.

"Follow me. Merlin, this way!" I call out as two teenage girls ride past on MagBoards. The girls turn their heads. Instead of snickering and pointing at me like I'm crazy, they wave their arms, helping guiding Merlin along. I smile, surprised. But, still, thank goodness the tide is low and the girls can't see Ollie bounding along beside me. That certainly would send them laughing. Snow White and her merry band. I'd have to make a run for it and hide.

People might make fun of you because they misunderstand you. What's not to understand? I'm weird. Different. Strange. But what if that's not so horrible?

I power on Sarafina and ramble a message off to Cora and Will to meet me at the Safe Haven. "I'll explain everything," I say, hoping they'll trust me enough to come. School will get out in a few minutes; I could check their location if I just turn on my FriendZ. But then I'd see all the hate posts. My finger trembles over the app. I flip my wrist and keep running.

"Should I notify Troy, tell him you're coming?" Sarafina asks.

"Yes. Good thinking." I don't want to overwhelm Troy. He's got enough going on while planning the move.

I duck around an apartment building. Along its side wall is a spray-painted image of a huge sun shooting golden arrows. Below is written:

Radiate your love.
Whatever you give your attention to
will grow stronger.

I feel my heart pumping oxygen and blood into my weary legs. Finally, the canals give way to the channel, the open waterway inside the marina that boats use to motor in and out of the ocean. As we near the docks, Ollie splashes. "Almost there?"

"Yes, but there's something I need to tell you." I grit my teeth and take a deep breath. "Misty has amnesia," I say. I tell him about the gash on her head and the loss of her sonar.

"I saw her being dragged, bleeding in those horrible nets," Ollie says with a tear in his eye. "I…I tried to free her." He gazes into the murky water. "I thought for certain she was dead. I cried for weeks and I swam crisscross around the islands searching for our pod. You see, earlier that day Nai'a—Misty, as you call her—and I went hunting on our own. We hadn't eaten in days, and we thought if we split up from the pod, we'd have better luck. Instead, I lost track of everyone."

"Wait! Did you and Misty go inside a cave?" I ask.

"Yes, and inside we found some crystals, but, no fish," Ollie says.

"Have you been back there?" I ask.

"No. And I'm never going back."

"Why not?"

"It was eerie and dark. I'm claustrophobic. I don't like being all closed-in like that. Misty led the way. But now you say she doesn't have sonar?"

I tell him about the vest we built her.

"So she can use it in the ocean when you set her free?"

My heart sinks. I tell him about Ocean World.

"Oh no!" Ollie gasps.

When we get to the dock at the Safe Haven, Merlin and Gabriella land on top of the rusty lanterns mounted on the pilings that hold the dock together. I head up to the deck.

Misty swims over. "I had this awful feeling you were never coming back for me," she says. "Where have you been?"

"I brought someone," I say.

"Who?"

"Give me a moment and I'll show you." I bang on the back door of the Ocean Lab. It swings open, and Troy stands in the doorway. Behind him are Cora and Will. I'm so relieved when I see them, I almost cry.

"What's going on?" Cora scolds, her arms folded. "I can't believe you called us here. Like you give a hoot about anything to do with the Safe Haven."

"Especially Misty," Will says, standing beside Cora. "To think I believed in you." He steps back.

"But I do care! I'm sorry. I was only thinking of myself. I didn't want to be different. I wanted to be popular, and I was afraid. Everything happened so fast. Georgia's party. All those followers on FriendZ. It was so much pressure. I had to keep wearing the vest. I mean, I didn't, but I did. It was wrong. I know that now."

"Why should we ever trust you again?" Will says.

Troy clears his throat, "Ah-hum." He strokes his goatee with raised eyebrows as he leans back against the newly repaired *KnifeFish*.

"Sorry about crashing it," I say, and finally fess up to him about how I stole the password. He shakes his head. "I know you're all mad, but please, we have to work together to free Misty." I tell them I brought her cousin.

"What? Where?" Cora brushes past me onto the deck.

Ollie whistles as I tell them all how he and the eagles found me at the beach. Gabriella and Merlin flap their wings. Misty swims across the pool to the edge closest to the dock. She slaps her tail and jumps into the air. Ollie squeals when he sees her. She whistles back.

"Tell them to free her," Ollie shouts anxiously from beneath the dock.

"Troy, please let Misty go," I plead. "Her cousin will take care of her. They have each other now."

"I can't monitor Misty out in the ocean like I can here. And, we're moving. I'm sorry! We're out of time."

My heart cringes with guilt. Oh, Mom!

Ollie squeals again louder.

"Well, if you won't let Misty out," I say, "how about letting Ollie into the pool?"

"Alright." Troy nods. "But just for a little while." He

admits the visit with family will do her good. He flips a switch and the steel gate between the pool and the water below the docks begins to lift. Ollie dives down and squeezes through. Suddenly, *screech*! The gate crashes down on him.

"Help! Help!" he yells, caught beneath the bars.

I swallow my breath and plunge into the water. I tug at the gate, but it doesn't budge. Bubbles rush out of my nose. I clamp my chest to hold on to the oxygen left in my lungs. Ollie squeals. Misty whistles and bumps into me. "Here, step on my tail," she says, giving me the leverage I need. I wrap my fingers around the bottom bar of the gate. As I push my feet down against her tail, I push up with my palms. The gate loosens. I jiggle it and keep pushing up with all my might. It lifts an inch, then two, then three more, and Ollie wriggles free. Misty nuzzles him with her snout. My heart soars, even as my lungs are about to burst. The dolphins twirl and swoop me up to the surface, where I gasp for air.

Will offers me his hand. "You okay?"

"I'm fine," I say, as I think about his mother drowning.

"You're really brave," he says to me, shaking his head.

"So are you," I say.

Troy hands me a towel.

"Maybe you have changed," Cora says.

I look into her eyes, then go to give her a hug, but she pulls away.

"You really hurt me," Cora says. "I thought we were best friends forever."

"I know. I'm sorry." I bow my head. I listen to Ollie and Misty's whistles and clicking back and forth at each other. I feel a nudge on my shoulder.

"You know," Cora says, "it's not too late. I have another computer chip. We can add satellite instead of cell coverage. Put it in Misty's vest. We'll be able to track her in open water."

"Like the chip that burned?" I can still smell the singe.

"Right. About that." Cora bites her lip. "I was just so mad at you! I couldn't stand watching you out there with Georgia, having fun while you lied to us. I revved the power to mess you up, but then the wiring must have short circuited."

"It's not your fault," I say and tell her how the vest probably slid because I never repaired the tear. Just like our friendship. "I really missed you," I say.

"Me too."

Afterward, as Cora upgrades Misty's vest, Troy suggests that the dolphins spend the night together in the tank.

"Oh, thank you!" I say. Wrapped in a towel, warmth

oozes from my heart. I watch Troy feed the dolphins a round of frozen mackerel. They gobble it up like a Thanksgiving feast.

"What about us?" Gabriella and Merlin squawk. Troy throws them each a fish too. He then looks over and smiles at me. But I know my work's not done—not yet. I still need to convince Troy to let Misty go free.

༄

That night Sarafina whispers in my ear. "There's a call coming in. It's Rebecca."

"What does she want?" I snap. Probably to ream into me about ruining our chances of ever winning the title. But I guess I've got to face her sooner or later. So, "Go ahead," I say. "Put her through."

"KyRose, I know why you did it. Why you wore the Echo Catcher," Rebecca says.

"You do?"

"Yeah! Georgia's so demanding. Everything's always gotta be *her way*. She only cares about her own victory."

"So then why have you been friends with her?" I ask.

"I thought I had to be," Rebecca says.

"Yeah, me too," I mumble.

"But you showed me another way."

"How? By cheating?"

"No! Through *The Zone*, silly! Ever since you told us about it, I've been singing a lot more and following my heart. I joined the chorus."

"You did? That's great! Congratulations. But that means you have to quit soccer."

"Yeah! I'm telling Georgia tomorrow. Coach Hartley called a pep rally even though it's Saturday. She's trying to pull some strings and said the team might be able to stay in the playoffs. But I don't care. I'm telling Georgia I quit. She won't be happy, but whatever. I'm done adapting to her every whim. I'm not gonna spend all of seventh grade worrying about *her*. I've got my own passions to chase."

Sarafina whispers in my ear, "I like this Rebecca."

"Hey, I owe you one," Rebecca says. "Call me anytime to repay the favor, okay?"

"Sure," I say. When we end the call, something occurs to me. I pull open my desk drawer. The rhinestones roll around. And there's the black glass—from the belly of the *KnifeFish*. I think about how precious they might be. The rhinestones I tack onto my lapel like a merit badge to remember I can always decorate myself without Georgia's approval. The piece of glass, I scan with my bracelet.

"Black crystal. Sarafina, what's that?" I ask, reading the results.

"It's an exceptionally rare crystal," she says, "known to be an energy source, only recently discovered on Earth. These crystals have been found in only three spots around the world, all near volcanos."

"Any in California?" I ask.

"There are no known deposits yet in or around California," she says.

"Well, then we just made a discovery!"

Early the next morning, I meet Cora and Will back at the Safe Haven. Through the windows of the Ocean Lab, I see Gabriella and Merlin gliding in circles above the docks. Below them is a skipper cleaning her boat. She calls out to another sailor beside her, who's getting ready to push off. Both sailors fling a loaf of bread up into the air. Merlin and Gabriella catch them. Guess the eagles have made new friends.

As soon as Ollie sees me, he swims over. "Misty's memory is back!" he exclaims, slapping his flippers.

Misty joins us. "I want to find my mother," she says.

I'm afraid to tell her that the pod is still nowhere to be found.

"Come on. We need to build your strength," Ollie says, and takes her for a lap around the pool.

Will shows me on the monitors how Misty's vitals are all up. "Pulse and body temperature are normal. Her depth perception is at 300%. That's got to be good, right?" he asks with a bounce in his step.

"Yes!" Troy says. "But we still need to keep an eye on her."

"Yeah, but we can watch her vitals and make sure her vest is working via satellite. Right?" I ask.

"Yep," Cora answers. Troy pats Cora on the back.

"So, problem solved. We can let her out!" I say.

"Only if it's safe?" Will asks concerned.

To test if Misty is strong enough to plow through the open waters, we all head onto the deck. I tell the others how her amnesia is lifted as Misty swims around the tank. Faster and faster. She then jumps up into the air and lands, splashing us. We all laugh. But when Misty jumps again, Merlin yells, "She's looking for another way out…to the ocean."

I grab the black crystal out of my pocket and show it to Misty. "Was it something like this that you had in your mouth that day when you later got caught in the nets?" I ask.

She gives the glassy crystal a lick. "Yes, that's it," she says.

Oh, I was so close, almost inside the cave with the *KnifeFish*. "Troy," I say, "Frankie missed something. Or maybe he found a totally different cave." I hold out the black crystal. Troy scans it through his tortoise scopes and confirms that it is the rare gem Sarafina said it was. "There's enough power just in this one crystal," he says, holding it up to the light, "to power not just the Safe Haven, but the entire marina for a week."

"Why don't we let the dolphins out to explore the

cave?" I suggest. "We can monitor Misty."

"Yeah, and track her remotely," Cora adds. "When she's in the ocean, you can collect even more data about how she's doing."

"It'll be a trial run," I say. "If all it goes well, we can set her free…forever."

"Then she and Ollie can find her mom," Will says, rubbing his eyes that look wet with tears.

"Troy, you said it yourself." I step forward. "Time's running out. Please, at least give her a chance," I plead.

"And risk losing her?" Troy shakes his head.

Ollie and Misty whistle.

"What are they saying?" Troy asks me.

"That it's a risk worth taking!"

Merlin and Gabriella recount the strange echoes coming from the shafts up by their nest. "We could fly down into the shafts," Merlin suggests. "Maybe they'll lead to that cave?"

I tell Troy how the eagles want to go too.

Then Troy, realizing he's been ambushed, shrugs. "Okay, okay." He leans back against the *KnifeFish*.

Cora's eyes twinkle. She looks at me, then at Will. "Are you thinking what I'm thinking?" she asks, tipping her chin toward the *KnifeFish*.

The three of us call out, all at the same time, "The ROVs!"

Twenty-four

The Real Mission

Cora, Will, and I mount the gyroscope cockpits in the Ocean Lab. Our newly delivered A/VR bodysuits—compliments of Cora's mom—fit us each like a glove.

"I'm excited," Cora says. "It'll be easy-schmeezy. No surprises, right?"

"Yep," I promise. No lies. "Just you and me—like old times. And Will and the animals, of course." Misty and Ollie left hours ago. So did Gabriella and Merlin.

"But that's it, no one else," Cora says, buckling in.

"It's going to be just like we said," I assure her. "A quick tour in the ROVs. We'll meet up with Misty and Ollie at Farnsworth Bank and track how well Misty does catching echoes with her vest."

"And to find those black crystals," Will says. He then

asks me, "Hey, is *your* vest working?"

Over my A/VR bodysuit, I'm wearing it. Will fixed it. He insisted—said we might need it to see our way in the dark down there. He replaced the burned-out nodes and printed another weave that's now cinched around my chest and back. I close my eyes. The nodes tingle, and everything in the lab comes into view: Cora and Will, the monitors on the wall, the aquariums in the far end of the room. I can even see the steel door that leads down the long hallway. I shoot Will a thumbs up.

Meanwhile, Troy hovers over his desk, twisting his fingers around the frames of his scopes. "Shoot! I can't find Frankie anywhere," he says. "I was hoping he'd go with you in his mini-sub." Troy peers up. "Oh well, guess you're on your own. KyRose, you have the *KnifeFish* again. It's almost at the island. Just be careful. Cost me quite a few LunaCoins to get all those dents out."

"Right," I say, and put on my helmet, embarrassed. Then my hands start trembling. "Sarafina, you there?" I whisper in a panic.

"Yes."

"Tell me again, why did I get stuck in the *KnifeFish* before? I should have been able to step right out of A/VR mode, no problem."

"It's highly probable that it was a clearance issue,"

Sarafina says. "The password you, well, stole...gave you control of the ROV, not the entire computer system. But want me to ask Troy?"

"No!" I won't let him scrub the mission. Misty and Ollie are counting on us.

"Well, don't worry," Sarafina says. "Troy gave me full access to the computer's operating system and the entire fleet of ROVs. I'll run system checks throughout the mission and make sure everything is working properly."

"Alright, fine," I say, breathing slowly, feeling a bit safer knowing my Amigo has our back.

Troy reads out the names of Will and Cora's ROVs. "The other two closest to the reef are *Manta Ray*. Will, I'm giving you that one. And, Cora, yours is *Calypso*."

"Hey, like Jacques Cousteau's research vessel." Cora smiles.

"Right! He was probably the most famous oceanographer ever," Troy remarks. "That could be you someday."

Will giggles. "Yeah, he was famous like you, KyRose."

"Not funny," I snap, and shoot him a sideways glance. "Fame is the last thing I want to chase right now!"

"That's just it," Troy says. "You don't have to chase it. All Jacques Cousteau did was follow his passion. He loved to explore the ocean, and when he shared his discoveries—the miraculous creatures and diversity under the water—people were in awe. They hadn't seen anything like that before. He opened their eyes. That's why he's famous."

"Sounds like a hero to me," Will says.

Hmm. I sit up and adjust the vest.

"Your ROVs are at the rendezvous spot. The dolphins are a kilometer away. Virtual mode is on. Ready to go?" Troy asks.

Cora, Will, and I all nod. We slip our gloves on, then slide the shields down on our helmets. The shields warp into A/VR headsets, gripped around our eyes. Inside, my dashboard lights up. Then my bodysuit triggers on. A second later, I'm transported. I feel cool water lapping against my skin.

"Cora, your mom rocks. These suits are amazing!" Will says as we float on the surface of the water. A view of Catalina Island, with its jagged cliffs, bobs up and down in the distance.

"Oh geez," Cora moans. "I think I'm gonna be seasick."

"I know. So real. And there's no way I can drown! Look, I'm a manta ray!" Will exclaims, and accelerates in a circle. "Woohoo!

"Watch out! You almost hit me!" Cora shouts, and banks right.

"Oops!" Will says. "Wow, look at all the buttons…Crane, Claw, Magnet, UV Lights, Camera, Lab. It's even got a Turbo Blast. Jammin'!"

Troy laughs. "Go on, have some fun. Press the buttons and take a practice run while you wait for the dolphins."

"KyRose, come on!" Will calls out. He's already four meters down, with Cora on his tail.

"You two go on. I'll wait here for Misty and Ollie."

There's not a cloud in the sky, so I dunk myself to cool off from the beating sun. Just as I pop up, I hear Will yell, "Help!"

"We're caught. Can't get out!" Cora shouts. "Aww, I'm gonna be sick."

"Hold on!" I turbo blast down and find the two ROVs spinning in a giant funnel. It's that undertow! It's back—and sucking my friends down fast. Quickly, I hit the Crane button and choose the Magnet tip. I line up beside the *Calypso*, just outside the wall of whirling water that looks like a tornado.

"What's going on?" Troy shouts.

"I got this!" I say. "Cora, I'm gonna lock on, then yank you out. Ready?"

"Hurry!" She gags. "I'm gonna puke."

I try, miss, and tumble back. I try again. Same thing happens. I inch closer, right up to the edge of the funnel. I feel the force trying to suck me in. I grip the handlebars and punch the Claw.

"Now!" I yell.

Clank!

"Gotcha!" But instantly, I'm flung sideways, spinning along with the *Calypso*. As hard as I can, I pull the handlebars in reverse and gun the turbo. Cora and I fly backwards. She's out, free.

"Thanks," Cora says as I race down to save Will.

When the three of us are back up at the surface, we use the ROVs' solar panels to charge up a bit. Fighting the undertow drained a lot of power from them.

That's when Will admits he was scared.

"Yeah, that was close," Cora says.

"Too close," Troy says, his voice strained. "We should abort the mission. At least, take you three off VR, and put the ROVs back on autopilot."

"But what about Ollie and Misty?" I ask. "If we go offline, I won't be able to talk to them."

Just then, Ollie pokes his head from the water. "Sorry it took us so long. Misty's a bit out of shape, you know. All that time in the tank." He chuckles, then stops, sensing something's wrong. "What happened?"

Before I can answer, Misty joins us, looking worn out. Troy reports her vitals are fine. Misty slaps her tail. "I might be tired, but I'm not giving up," she says, and dives down. Ollie follows her.

"Troy, please. I have to go after them. I promised to

keep them safe."

"We're coming with you." Will spins the *Manta Ray*, ready to dive again.

"Definitely!" Cora adds, moving the *Calypso* closer.

Troy gives in. "But if it gets rough again, you're out. I'm pulling you all offline."

"Ay ay, captain!" I say, and the three of us duck after the dolphins.

As we descend, I show Cora and Will how to draft—like the eagles—to save energy. We take turns leading. At first, everything around us looks familiar…spiny coral billowing in the shelves of rock, tiny fish darting into crevices. But, halfway to the bottom, I see something I hadn't seen before: a pink cloud. It resembles a nebula, like in outer space—past Mars, even Pluto—with gas and dust that acts as a nursery for new stars. But it's here on Earth, hidden in the sea—a colony of millions of phytoplankton. The pink cloud is made up of microscopic life, dancing and twirling in the last reaches of sunlight. Around this plume of phytoplankton is another swirl. It's zooplankton feeding on the phytoplankton. And, there's yet another layer swarming around the outer edges: rose-colored krill feasting on the zooplankton. All together it's the circle of life come alive.

"Can you smell us? Can you see me?" I ask the tiny creatures. I don't expect an answer. But by the thousands, they huddle in a ball. I feel their tiny hearts beat like raindrops. A school of minnows race over to nibble on the krill. My fingers tingle. "Troy, the ecosystem! It's back!" And, I know it's true because a school of mackerel swim past us, chasing after the minnows.

"Resilience. That's the beauty of life. Always adapting," Troy says. "It's what makes us each unique."

So we *are* all special! Even me.

"And we each have a role to play," Troy adds. Ollie snaps at a fish, missing. The mackerel flit off.

"Not now," Misty scolds. "Lunch will have to wait." She slips down between the coral shelves. We turn on our spotlights and follow her, deeper and deeper until…finally, we face the mouth of the eerie, dark cave.

I shiver, remembering my last episode here. "Sarafina, is there going to be another undertow?" I ask, gripping the handlebars.

"I've been timing the currents. They come in bursts from the cave every eight minutes and fifty-two seconds," Sarafina says.

I fire high frequency clicks into the cave. The sound waves rebound and the nodes streak across my back. Instantly, my mind draws an image. A long, winding tunnel with walls covered in sharp barnacles.

"I'll lead the way," I say, trembling.

"It's okay. We're right behind you," Misty says,

sensing my fear.

With my gloved finger, I rub the wings of my necklace. *Trust in the mystery of the unknown. Step bravely forward.* I take a deep breath. Sarafina counts the seconds then tells us when to go. With a leap of faith, I lead us…slowly into the darkness.

Twenty-five
Behind the Veil

Single-file, we twist and turn through the narrow labyrinth of the tunnel. Barnacles, all around us, look like dotted craters on the moon. Their shells are glued like cement onto the walls and their feathery legs are out probing—filtering the water—to catch tiny morsels of food. We creep deeper in. Our ROVs' headlights dimly light the way, and their sensors relay signals onto our dashboards. Even so, *Ska-reech*! The *Calypso* scrapes against the barnacles.

"Oops," Cora says.

"Stay on my tail," I say, and shoot sound waves up ahead. "A few more turns. We're almost there."

Finally, the tunnel walls give way to an opening. We arrive in the belly of an aqua blue pool. With water above and below us, the pool reaches as wide as a soccer field.

Cora peers over the ledge with the *Calypso*.

"Stay back," I warn. "We need to get a better look *before* we head in."

Will points up with the *Manta Ray's* crane. The surface above is blurry.

"There's a pocket of air up there," I say, zooming in. The ceiling is rugged with hundreds of daggers hanging low. "Troy, you getting this?"

"Yeah. The cave must be made of limestone, carved out millions of years ago."

"From a volcano?!" I spew, remembering what Sarafina said about black crystals only being discovered near volcanos that have erupted.

"Yes, very likely," Troy says. "And, see those stalactites," he says, explaining the daggers on the ceiling. "Those are formed by minerals dripping off the rocks for thousands of years."

Droplets teeter on the tips of the daggers until they drip like rain onto the surface of the water. Ripples grow wide…then scatter, bump, and merge into one another. They wash onto the shore of a pebbled beach that's at the far corner of the cave. A howling comes from the corner. *Whoosshh!* It passes like wind through a flute. I blast a sound wave and see an airshaft. Sarafina explains it's a volcanic vent that must have once carried lava up to the surface. I can see the airshaft pipe up like a chimney, all the way to the sky. Oh my gosh! Gabriella and Merlin were right! Maybe, they will find their way here.

I tell the others, as Cora scoops up a sample of water. She uses the *Calypso's* onboard lab to test it. "Contains nitrogen, iron ore, calcium carbonate, rhyolite, and there's platinum too," she says.

"Huh? A treasure trove," Troy says, surprised, as though he didn't believe our hunch about the place.

"What about black crystals?" I ask.

Sarafina answers. I put her on intercom so Cora, Will, and Troy can hear what she has to say. "The bonded structure of the crystals includes all those minerals Cora just found. So, it is highly probable—"

"Yeah, yeah. We know they're here. But where?" I cut her off and anxiously look around. Below us, the pool dips twenty feet. The sandy bottom whisks around like a desert storm. The dolphins and I blast sound waves, but can't see much through the cloudy murk.

Misty then points with her snout. "There's something down there."

"Look!" Ollie points to a curved shadow. It slashes through the murk, then disappears.

"And over here!" Will calls out, pointing twenty degrees to the left. "Looks like a tail!"

"And a snout!" Cora yelps. "And look there, a fin!"

The shapes come together. "Dolphins!"

"You're kidding," Troy says.

Will counts them aloud. "One, two, three…seven…twelve…eighteen. There's twenty of 'em!"

"Our pod!" Misty shouts. "Mama! I'm here." She races down. Ollie follows.

"Wait!" I call after them.

"Let 'em go. She found her mom!" Wills says, choked up, like he's about to cry.

Cora taps me on the shoulder with her claw. "Is he okay?" she whispers.

My heart swells. I feel Will's pain…and the love for his mom. "Yeah, I think so," I whisper back.

We listen in silence to the trills and whistles of Misty and Ollie as they disappear completely into the clouds of sand.

"I can't believe we found their pod here," I say.

"Look at the way the dolphins are fanning their bodies," Cora says. "What's that all about?"

"It's like they're digging," I say.

"Yeah, but for what?" Will asks, catching his breath. "And what's that over there?" He points to a red bucket at the other end of the pool. The bucket hangs from the end of a rope. A dolphin swims toward it. The dolphin's eyes are strangely glazed, milky white. It opens its mouth over the bucket, and out falls a plum-sized stone.

"What? Could that be…a black crystal?" Will whispers.

"That's it!" Cora shouts. "They're mining for gems!"

"But how would they know about crystals?" Will asks.

With my camera, I zoom in on the dolphin by the bucket. "Look!" I shout. Clipped to its head is a metal disc with a blinking purple light.

I gasp!

"*Think-It*?!" Cora says with horror.

"Someone's controlling the dolphins' brains!" I yelp. Then I remember the hacker on the news. What if it's them? "They stole Think-It to use on the dolphins."

"Like slaves," Wills says.

"Or zombies!" I shout. Dad was right. My chest burns. We have to do something. "The ancient Greeks would throw criminals like these into jail!" I rant.

"Yeah!" Will says. "But is it even illegal? I mean, do we have laws to protect animals from something like *this*?"

"If we don't," Cora blusters, "and Rachel Carson were still alive, well, she'd go straight to Congress and tell those law makers to change the law."

"That's right!" I say, fuming, and for a second, I imagine myself marching up the steps of Capitol Hill in Washington, D.C. "This is animal abuse! No one should mind control others with technology. Not ever. Especially without their permission."

"I'm calling the Coast Guard right now!" Troy says.

Just then, an alarm rings inside the lab. *Breep-Breep. Breep-Breep.* It blares like one of those fire drills at school.

"That's strange. I don't smell smoke," Troy says. "I'll be right back." His chair rolls across the floor. I hear his footsteps. The door creaks open, then slams shut behind him. Seconds later, the ringing stops. But it's followed by a pounding.

"Troy, you okay?" I call out.

"He's locked outside, in the hallway," Sarafina says. I remember the two doors—one at each end of the corridor. "You don't mean *both* doors are locked?"

"Yes, he's trapped inside," Sarafina says.

Troy keeps pounding.

"Well, get him out!" I order.

"No need to yell at me," she says. I guess her emotions are turned up again.

"I'm sorry. Just please, do it," I say.

"I'm trying. Automated systems are malfunctioning..." Static on the line breaks up her words.

Alright! I'll do it myself. I reach to pull off my headset, but stop when I hear a strange voice echo through the cave.

"You're not going anywhere!"

"Who's there?" Will asks.

"You shouldn't have come!" the voice grates. From the husky tone, I can tell it's a man's voice. He goes on, "Couldn't take a hint, could ya? I don't want to hurt you kids. Just stay out of my way!" Beneath the gruff tone, the voice sounds vaguely familiar.

"We're not scared of you," Cora calls out.

The three of us swim from the ledge out into the center of the pool. We spin our ROVs, searching all angles. Meanwhile, Troy keeps pounding on the door.

"Show yourself!" I call out. But there's only us and the dolphins below. I blast more sound waves. Beyond the pebbled beach, past the airshaft, I see a slit in the rocks that I hadn't seen before. The opening is narrow and runs deep like an iceberg. A light flickers, reflecting on jagged walls around it. I steer the *KnifeFish* and come up beneath the opening. I can't believe my eyes.

A single capsule submarine. Inside, a dark figure sits scrunched up behind the bubble glass. I see the propeller and then the name written across the sub.

"Frankie?!" I blurt, stunned.

Cora and Will swim up beside me.

"What? You're the one behind this?" Cora sputters.

Will bangs his fist.

Frankie sighs. "Look, just forget you saw me," he says softly.

"Forget we saw you?? We trusted you," I say. "Why

would you do such a thing?" My shoulders slump.

"Hey look, I got the idea from the U.S. Navy," Frankie says. "They trained dolphins to find mines underwater. And those were the kind that go boom. This ain't nearly as bad."

"Crystals might not explode, but pricking the dolphins' brains? That's not *bad*?" Will spats.

"Fine!" Frankie says. "But I had to do it. After I, well, messed up and things got out of hand."

"What do you mean?" Cora asks.

"There were plenty of fish for Pops when my invention worked like a charm," Frankie says.

"You mean that gadget that you pointed in the water?" Will asks.

"Your *electromagnetic field generator*. Of course!" I say, remembering the plaque. "You played with the Earth's magnetic field. Tricked the mackerel to come right up to your boat. They must have thought they were headed north, but swam here to the islands instead. That's why they showed up in droves. And the great migration followed. That's all because of you?!"

"Yeah. Yeah. Every big fish and its brother came and stole our catch. I wasn't counting on that! And those damn eagles, they were the worst," Frankie says, wagging the throttle, sending the sub thudding side to side.

"Hey! Those are my friends, and they were here

first!" I say, toughening up.

"Yeah. Yeah. I know," Frankie says. "And the ecosystem went bust—all because of me. I never meant for it to go that far. Like I said, things…got out of hand."

"And now the eagles are starving because of you," I say, angrily.

"I'm sorry!" Frankie hails. "I have to take care of Pops. He's getting old and owning a fish farm would be a lot easier than fishing out on that scrappy *Maiden Voyage*, and he'd always have a steady supply of fish."

Will points to a pouch that sags from the underbelly of the sub. "There must be one hundred kilos of crystals in there," he says. "You're planning to sell them and use the money to buy a fish farm?"

Frankie cinches the pouch tight. "That's right! They're mine. And crystals don't pollute— no oil leaks or carbon released into the earth's atmosphere. Lucky for me, I found 'em."

"You mean Misty found them, and you pulled it out of her mouth," I say. "Then tracked the currents and found her path here…to the cave. You already knew about this place when I first asked you? Didn't you?"

Frankie huffs without a word.

"And the currents," Cora says. "I bet that's how you got the idea to make the undertow?"

"You kids are clever, aren't ya?" Frankie says with a huff. "I had to protect my treasure!"

"Well, you know what's *not* clever?" I say, my heart pumping. "Animal abuse!"

"Frankie, you could use tech for good instead!" Will says.

"Wait 'til Troy finds out!" Cora chimes in. "We know you locked him in that hallway. Now let him out."

"No way!" Frankie says. "He'll never find out it was me. I'm gonna wipe the computers clean. I'll be out of here with the crystals. There won't be evidence, not a trace, left of me."

"Oh yeah? Well, we're gonna tell him. We're gonna tell everyone," Will says, inching closer to the sub.

"No one's gonna believe you. You're just kids. And everyone knows, kids lie. Isn't that right, KyRose?" Frankie's words hit me like a punch in the stomach.

"You won't get away with it!" Will blares.

"Yeah, and who's gonna stop me?" Frankie snaps, losing his patience.

Will reaches with his crane. Frankie pulses an undertow out of the sub's propeller and flings the *Manta Ray* back down.

"It doesn't matter," Cora says. "The Coast Guard. They're on their way."

"Oh, please. I intercepted that call. No one is coming," Frankie says.

"Sarafina, is that true?" I ask desperately. But all I hear is static on the line.

"Yeah, your Amigo ain't gonna help ya either. Now I just need a few more crystals, and I'll be on my way." Frankie cranks the rope and empties the bucket into the pouch beneath the sub. "Oh, and thanks for bringing me two extra dolphins," he says. "Now, stay out of my way!"

"Misty and Ollie—where are they?" Will panics.

I call out to them.

Misty whistles back. "We're down here. Help!" Twenty feet below us, five zombie dolphins have her and Ollie pressed up against a wall.

"Will, Cora, come on." I lead them down. "We have to do something!"

"I warned you," Frankie snarls. "Hope you're wearing your seatbelts." He triggers an undertow. It hurls me into a nosedive. *Bam*! I crash to the bottom, stuck in a mound of sand. Dizzy, I shake my head and call out to Cora and Will. No answer. That's enough! This A/VR ride is over. I reach to yank off my headset, but my hands are stuck—glued to the handlebars.

Twenty-six
True Leap

I'm still stuck at the bottom of the cave. My gloves won't budge off the handlebars. I wriggle my fingers, but the gloves are cinched too tight. I can't get my hands to move. The sand around me grows thicker as dolphins keep digging. I try my headlights. Nothing happens. They must have busted in the crash. Luckily, my vest still works.

I shoot sound waves. On the ledge of the tunnel, I see the *Manta Ray* and the *Calypso* flipped upside down. The ROVs teeter on the edge. They must have been swept there in the undertow Frankie shot at us.

I call out, "Cora? Will?"

They moan as if their mouths are taped shut, and struggle, rocking back and forth.

"Stop. You'll fall," I yell. "Sarafina! Do something! Please!!!"

The static on the line is gone. Maybe because Frankie is fast at work, focused on getting the last of the crystals, his guard is down.

Sarafina answers. "He has full control of the computers," she whispers. "We're all locked in. No way out."

"Sarafina! You promised this wouldn't happen again!"

"I'm sorry. He's encrypted the code. I'm scanning for a loophole to get you kids out of there. But I need more time."

"Hurry!" Adrenaline floods my chest. I blast more sound waves and see Misty and Ollie still held up against the wall. A fisheye robot covered in spikes like a blowfish lowers from the sub. The robot aims first for Ollie. Inches from his skull, the robot's spikes begin to turn. They're needles that will drill in and poke electrodes into his brain. The zombie dolphins follow their orders. They hold him down, as Ollie struggles with all his might.

"Sarafina! Quick!"

"I've got an open line. It's private. Frankie won't hear. Who should I cam?"

"Rebecca!" I need that favor now!

A second later, she's on the line. I hear drumming

and kids hollering in the background at the pep rally.

"Hey, KyRose," Rebecca says. "I told Georgia I quit the team. Dang, is she mad." Her gaze veers off screen, then, back at me. "Uhh...she wants to talk to you," Rebecca says.

"No! Not now! I need your help."

Too late, Georgia shimmies in front of the camera. "What? Too busy for an old friend?" She leans in, her lone-wolf eyes steamy and wide. "*You* tried to ruin me, you fake! We almost got kicked out of the playoffs. Now you're gonna pay." She twists her lips and backs away as Rex, Dante, and Avery gather round.

I hear a tap. Then a red square pops up onto the screen.

"Sarafina! What just happened?"

"Georgia is live streaming," Sarafina says.

I reel, dizzy. Then jerk my hands, but they're still stuck. "How many viewers?" I ask, trying not to bark at Sarafina.

"There are 909 viewers...make that 912," Sarafina says.

"And Frankie has no idea we're being streamed? I ask.

"Go on, Snow White," Georgia taunts. "Show us how you talk to animals...*for real*. You weirdo." She cackles. My heart pounds. I wish I had a chance to tell her the truth. I really do. Like Rebecca, I want to come clean. But now, with everyone watching, I freeze. Then Georgia says, "Let's make it more fun." She tells Dante and Rex to broadcast the stream on their *Smash Spectator* feeds. The boys' arms reach across the screen.

"That'll be another 100,000 viewers," Rebecca yelps. Tabeen pokes her head in for a glimpse. A second later, the numbers vault.

"25,022 viewers now, and counting," Sarafina says.

A spectacle. I'm just someone to laugh at! *Liar, liar, vest on fire*...the chant echoes in my head. It pounds my temples and grips the backs of my eyes. My chest rises, and the fear floods in. Oh, Abuela, wherever you are...help! I can't breathe. My mind races back to everything I did *wrong* to fit in and *to be liked*. The lies I told, the way I shut out Gabriella and Merlin, and how I hid my truth. But do I have the courage now? Can I show the world who I am?

"Step into *The Zone*," Rebecca says. Her words flutter like butterflies. They spiral and vibrate. My necklace tingles.

Still, all I want to do is tell Sarafina to drop the line, end the cam. Just then, my hands break free.

"KyRose, I cracked the code," Sarafina says. "You, Cora, and Will can take off your headsets and walk away."

Ollie squeals. The needles drill into his head.

My gut flutters. No, we're not abandoning the

animals! I don't care who sees me.

"Frankie, stop!" I shout.

"Come on, everyone knows that humans rule the planet," Frankie's voice echoes for all to hear.

"You're wrong. Humans are a part of nature. And animals have rights!" I say. "They're intelligent. We need to use our tech to learn from them, not enslave them to do our dirty work." I flip my camera onto the dolphins and the robot with needles.

Rebecca and Tabeen gasp.

"And those black crystals, they belong to Catalina!" I zoom in on the sub.

"Oh, shut up! The crystals are mine. Now, stop meddling," Frankie shouts.

Just then, I see *wings* swoop down through the airshaft.

"See! I told you we'd find her," Gabriella says.

"Yeah, then where is she?" Merlin asks.

"I'm down here!" I yell, but they can't hear me. I'm too deep in the water. I rev my engine and break free from the sand. I race up with the *KnifeFish*.

"Quick, eagles, stop that sub!" I yell.

Gabriella and Merlin dive bomb Frankie's submarine, scratching and pecking at the bubble glass. Frankie dodges the sub, trying to get away.

On the screen, Avery, Rex, and Dillon's mouths all fall open. "Oh my gosh! She really can talk to animals!"

Avery says.

In the background, I hear Rebecca and Sarafina share whispers.

I turn the *KnifeFish* back down. "Misty! Ollie! I'm coming," I shout.

"We're all coming," Rebecca calls, and bolts off screen. Tabeen, Rex, and Dillon dash after her.

Georgia spins around. "Hey! Where are you all going?"

"To the FabLab! And then the library! Quick! Come on!" I swear it's Avery's voice that says it.

Minutes later, a fleet of five ROVs careen through the tunnel and into the cave.

"KyRose, it's me, Rebecca." She glides over in a ROV called the *Electric Eel*. "Tabeen, Rex, and Dillon…we're all here. Even Avery. And we've got our Mars gadgets uploaded, thanks to your Amigo," Rebecca explains.

I can't believe my eyes. "Wait! Sarafina? Did you just break the rules?"

"Let's just say I had a feeling about bending them a bit," she says.

Rex snaps his crane. Using Mabel's beak power, he flips *Calypso* and the *Manta Ray* upright. Rebecca then gives them a jolt of energy from her Eel Battery Pack. Cora and Will start their engines.

"Thank goodness you're okay," I say to Cora and Will.

"So much for easy-schmeezy," Cora says.

"I know! This has been a lot of drama. You okay?" I ask.

"Definitely!" Cora perks up and spins *Calypso* around so she can see all the ROVs working together as a team. "We got this! Let's go!" she says.

"Free the dolphins!" I shout.

Rex and Rebecca swim into the sand storm and start to unclip the mind controlling implants from the dolphins one by one. Will, Cora, and I rush over to Misty and Ollie. I give the fisheye robot a swift kick, and Will dunks it into the red bucket, where it squirts, all berserk. We high-five with our cranes, then remove the implants from the zombie dolphins that press on Misty and Ollie. Cora frees Ollie, and Misty hugs her mom, whose eyes have returned back to normal.

Meanwhile, Tabeen jets up near the sub. She uses the vacuumed-up plastic in the belly of her ROV to spin a web. It comes out a rainbow color. She casts it over the pouch of crystals, then weaves a second net. "Here! Grab this," she says to Gabriella and Merlin. Remarkably, they seem to understand her, and grab hold of it with their claws. Together with Tabeen, they snare the sub.

"We got him!" Tabeen shouts.

"Frankie, you ready to give up now?" Merlin shouts. I translate, but Frankie revs his engine instead, still trying to make a run for it.

Avery motors over calling out to Dillion, "Get ready!" She uses the mantis shrimp goggles to spot the engine of the sub with all its sparks. She points it out to Dillon, who punches it with bullet speed and a mantis kick. The engine creeps to a halt. Dillon punches again, this time at the propeller, leaving it dented once again.

Frankie lasers a hole through the nets and jumps out of the sub. He crawls onto the pebbled beach, then he climbs up the airshaft. Seconds later, he comes tumbling down. Hundreds of drones chase after him. They bang into his head, one after the other…racking up *Smash Spectator* points.

Frankie wraps his arms, trying to shield his head. He cries out, "Make them stop!"

"Now, you know what it feels like to be attacked by technology," I say.

Later, when the dolphins are free, they swim up to the pebbled beach where Frankie sits hunched over. Misty and her mother snuggle and kiss.

Frankie watches them, bowing his head. "I just wanted to help Pops," he says. "I messed up. I'm sorry."

Misty whistles at him.

"She might be willing to forgive you," I say.

"But why? After all I've done."

"Because she knows…we all make mistakes," I say,

and look over at Cora. She give me a thumbs up with her crane.

Frankie goes on to apologize to Merlin and Gabriella and all the dolphins one by one. He then reaches his hand out to Misty. She slaps the water with her tail splashing Frankie in the face, but Frankie keeps his hand held out. Misty looks back at her mother, then at Ollie and the rest of her pod. She swims around making sure they're all okay. Then, finally, she inches towards Frankie and lets him pet her softly on her melon.

With my headset still on, I grin into the camera. The live stream is still going—over two million viewers watching. "To everyone out there," I say in a clear voice. "My name is KyRose Sanchez and I talk to animals. I once tried to hide that, but now I know we're all meant to be *different*. It's how we survive, and it's what makes us stronger as an ecosystem. Each living being has a power and a special way of seeing the world that's unique. Animals want to survive, just like you and me, with clean water, fresh air, healthy food, a safe place to live…oh, and lots of love, of course. Thanks everyone, for coming together to help us! Keep it going. Take a stand for animals and nature everywhere. After all, we *all* belong to this planet. And if we stop, listen, and watch closely, we might even see a whole new world through the eyes of animals…and their senses."

That's when Puddles jumps on my lap.

Twenty-seven

Home

"I can't believe it was him!" Troy says.

Cora, Will, and I are still at the Safe Haven in the Ocean Biome. On the monitors, we watch the Coast Guard take Frankie into custody. Thousands of drones buzz across the sky. Together, they form the shape of an eagle, wings flapping in the air.

"Now *that's* synchronicity," Rebecca says over the line. She's in the library at MakerX20.

"I can't thank you enough for your help. All of you," I say.

"Are you kidding? We wouldn't have missed it for the world," Rebecca says, patting Rex on the shoulder.

"That's right!" Rex says. He, Tabeen, Rebecca, Avery, and Dillon all high-five.

"Have you seen Georgia?" I ask.

"She ran out in a huff. I don't think we'll see much of her this week," Avery says with a shrug.

"KyRose, you're coming back to school, right?" Tabeen asks.

"She sure is," Dad answers for me. He leans over Puddles and gives me a kiss. Mom's out the deck, pacing with her scopes on. She points at the Oyster Village, then to the boats in their slips, and then back over toward us.

"So, KyRose, that means you'll be at Exhibition Day on Thursday!" Rebecca says, pulling my attention back to the conversation.

"Friends and family are invited," Cora adds. "Troy, you have to come."

"I don't know! I've got a lot of work. Gotta pack up the Safe Haven for our move."

Just then, Mom walks in. "Oh, sweetheart, I'm so proud of you. Talk about kid power!" Mom says. Then she whispers something more into my ear.

"And, your boss didn't fire you?!" I yelp, and jump up with joy. "Everyone, listen up! Tell 'em, Mom."

"Well," she says. "Clearly, Troy, you're doing incredible work here. We can't just push you out when we could team up with you instead. The rest of the idea I got from KyRose. With self-driving cars shuttling people around these days, you don't need that big parking lot out front. I told my boss, 'Agree or I'm out.'" Mom winks at me. "So, Troy, if it's okay with you, we'll put our gaming arena in your parking lot. You can stay in this building, and we'll make a walkway along the water to connect the Oyster Village to the Safe Haven. Visitors will be able walk back and forth so they can see all the incredible animals—and their *superpowers*. They can also learn about what they can do to keep the oceans clean and provide healthy habitats for all of us. Sound good?"

We all cheer!

"That's awesome, Mrs. Sanchez. Thank you!" Troy says.

"Call me Renee," Mom says, and gives Troy a hug.

At Exhibition Day, we showcase our final projects. I wear my old khaki tee, but along the chest pocket are rhinestones I added as decoration. The hallways of MakerX20 are bustling with students, teachers, parents, and friends. *Mission Columbia* is set to land on Mars in just twelve days. Mr. Bracket makes an announcement, then puts up the broadcast from space. Astronauts' faces pop onto all the digital posters, monitors, and banners that hang in the halls.

"We used our 3D printers," Captain Marco says, holding up a duplicate of both Rex's Snapper Beak and our Echo Catcher. "Once we land on Mars, we'll give your inventions a try. Though we heard you already put them to good use on Earth! To all you kids out there, keep tinkering! We need all of your inventions."

There's a round of applause. Mom and Dad give me a big hug. I look over at Will. He's happy we got to be a finalist for the GoMars contest, but more than that, Will is at ease. He let go of the blame for his mom's accident. His father stands next to him now. Will squeezes his hand and smiles up at him. They hug, and I feel the room get warm. I wonder if his mom's spirit and Abuela's are together, and what they might be wishing for us.

Across the way, up on a wall I read a quote:

> "Ultimately, the two most important questions
> to ask yourself in the search for your **passion** are:
> **what do you love?** and **what do you love about it?**
> —Sir Ken Robinson

Cora and I place a platform at the center of our booth. On top of it, Will sets the mannequin that models the Echo Catcher. Kids crane their necks for a better look.

Someone yells out, "Hey, Snow White, give us a demo."

I smile. I have to admit, she is my favorite princess!

Then someone else shouts, "Does it work just like

on the FriendZ stream?"

Cora, Will, and I share a knowing smile. I put on the vest. Will powers it up. I slip the headband over my third eye. I wear it inside out this time so everyone can see the emitter. Cora turns on a projector that shows the nodes lighting up across my back. She then plays an animation of the impulses being sent to my brain, my neurons firing. I close my eyes and watch as the room falls into view.

At the end of the hall, through a sea of people, I spot Jack and Emily. I wave at them. Jack waves back as he puts his other arm around Emily. He really does like her. I guess I'm okay with it. I mean, Jack will always be my brother. Emily teases him, points her camera first at him, then swings it around at me. She snaps a video. I pose sideways to be sure the vest is showing. Jack calls out, "Way to go, sis!" and flips me a proud thumbs up!

As I look around, I see Rebecca activate her Eel Battery Pack. She and her teammates fire lightning bolts into a glass cylinder. At the same time, they sing out the sound effects for thunder. At the next booth over, Tabeen demos her spider suit. She's played around with the design again. It was her thirteenth birthday two days ago. Over the bodysuit, she wears a long dress with a matching hijab headscarf. "On Mars, and on Earth, I can be glamorous," she says and spins around. Her mom, wrapped in her own headscarf, stands beside her father, whose rolled cuffs are stitched with little rainbows. The two nod applauding their fashionista daughter with beaming smiles.

At the other end of the hall, Avery and the twins have a group giggling as Dillon crawls on the floor with their Mantis Kicker. He's got the goggles on too. The frames are still red, but covered in light blue polka dots. I'm glad to see that Georgia and Avery were able to make a compromise.

By the trophy case, Ms. A chats with the mayor of Catalina. Troy shakes the Mayor's hand. Yesterday, she granted the Safe Haven a reward of 300,000 LunaCoins. The recovered black crystals were estimated to be worth fifty times that. Troy offered Captain Maloney most of the reward money to buy the *Maiden Voyage*. Troy is going to fix it up and turn it into a research vessel. The captain decided to retire instead of buying a fish farm. He was super distraught over the lengths Frankie went to try and take care of him, but love and loyalty rule, and father and son made up pretty quickly.

Meanwhile, Mom offered Troy help with the paperwork to buy the boat and other stuff he needs around the Safe Haven. In exchange, Troy is helping her with an idea she had using biomimicry. Oysters, like barnacles, filter water, and Mom wants to use a similar design to filter all the water fountains at the Oyster Village, as well as the water out in the marina to keep it clean. So, it really will be an Oyster Village.

Cora, Will, and I also met with the mayor of Catalina. We explained everything that Frankie had done, including messing up the migration patterns of the fish that led to overfishing. The mayor declared the water around the Channel Islands a Fish Reserve. Now the ecosystem will definitely have a chance to fully recover, and Gabriella and Merlin will be able to breed and feed their chicks. Fishermen are only allowed to fish on the outskirts of the Reserve. Troy and Sarafina gathered a bunch of data. It shows how plenty of fish spill out of the reserved area, so fishermen can keep their livelihood, and overfishing won't ever be a problem again. It's a win-win for everyone. And when I say *everyone*, I mean the animals too, of course!

As for Frankie, Troy actually offered him a job…to install and maintain gear on the *Maiden Voyage* research vessel. Frankie was grateful for the job, and their friendship. He'll start once he completes the 1,000 hours of community service that the mayor said he had to do. Part of those hours will be spent writing a new bill to protect the rights of animals. Also, the MetaTech company agreed not to press criminal charges against Frankie, as long as he agreed to do a job for them. I guess they figured that if Frankie could break into their cybersecurity system and steal the Think-It code, who better to re-program it and design a foolproof system to stop future intruders?

Oh, and Troy said he'd use the last of the reward money to reintroduce more animals into the wild. Mabel is slated to go first, back to Costa Rica next month.

When the mayor walks off, Ms. A pulls out the pin that holds up her hair. She leans up and kisses Troy, smack on the lips. Wow! It's nice to see Ms. A easygoing and happy.

Later, when we get home, Mom and Alfred make tea and sandwiches together for all of us. Will and his father are here too. Mom invited them over, and she already asked them to come back for Thanksgiving dinner next month.

That night in the kitchen, Dad pulls down a jar of Abuela's seeds. "I'll plant these in the morning," he says. "Beside her roses." Then he uncorks a bottle of nut oil. "This just arrived," he says. "It's picked, pressed, and manufactured by locals in the Amazon Rainforest. It's sustainably made, and I want to support them from now on!" Dad pours a shot of the oil into his new juice concoction, then pours a second shot into a tin can with a skinny spout. He tips the can and oils the springs in Alfred's joints. When he's done, Dad pats Alfred on the back and says, "Mira, you're part of the family now."

Alfred's eyes light up. He plays music (which we had no idea he could do), and Mom and Dad dance in the kitchen.

~

The following week, the Jaguars play in the championship girls soccer game. I sit with Cora and Will on the bleachers. Tabeen runs up and tosses me a green shirt. I had given her the dress Abuela made me, the one I outgrew. Tabeen cut it and sewed it together as a new tee.

"Thanks," I say.

"Check out the back," Tabeen says.

I hold it up. Embroidered with gold thread are a pair of wings.

"So you can soar," she calls out as she runs back onto the field.

As we wait for the game to begin, I show Cora and Will the flurry of clips on my FriendZ feed. There's been over 70,000 posted from kids around the globe, ever since Misty, Ollie, and the pod were rescued. Even Chandelle Waterhouse—I couldn't believe it—sent me a message saying that *I* inspire *her*. With it were squiggly hearts and clapping hand emojis.

Miriam walks up the bleachers. She looks around for a place to sit, about to pass by us.

"Wanna sit here?" I ask.

She smiles, and I scoot over to make room for her.

I then tap the latest post on my feed. We all look over at my bracelet as the video plays.

"Hi. My name is Lauren. I know lots of people have stopped using plastic bags, but lately there's been a lot passing through the storm drains in my hometown of Singer Island, Florida." Her video cuts to the ocean. "Here in the Atlantic," she says, "bags float forever." The video cuts again to a bag the size of a dinner plate. Its edges are bitten away. "Small fish mistake it for food," Lauren says. She then zooms in with a microscopic lens. Up close, we see shellfish and tiny plankton clinging to the bag. "This is where they've made their home...but shouldn't they be using something more natural, like driftwood? Can you help?"

"We should ban plastic bags forever!" Cora says.

"Or make them out of kelp," Will adds.

"Wouldn't it be awesome? Helping kids around the world solve crimes against nature?" I say.

"And, we can all be friends," Skinner says, hopping onto my shoulder. "Uhh, do you have any nuts?"

I giggle as Cora beats me to the punch and pulls a walnut from her bag. I watch as she busts it open.

"Hey, I know, let's call ourselves The Buster Club!" I exclaim.

Sarafina chimes in. "Your heart is beating fast. I think you're onto something."

"Oh, and we'll only bend the rules, not break them," I say, and Sarafina giggles.

I rub my necklace and think of how proud Abuela

would be if we *did* start The Buster Club. But it could be a lot of responsibility. Could I lead the team? Just then, a flock of ravens fly overhead. They caw and land on the canopy of the oak trees. I squeeze my necklace and make a wish.

Before the kickoff, Rebecca sings the national anthem.

"Wow, she's got a strong and gorgeous voice," Cora says.

"Yeah, maybe she'll sing at our Halloween party?" I say with a wink. Mom and Dad said we could have it at our house. I hope they don't freak out when they see how many kids we've invited.

Right as the game starts, Will moves up two rows…to play *Smash Spectator* with Rex and Dillon. Dante sits a row behind him. He pokes Will's shoulder.

"Hey, I'm really sorry about what I said…about you being a mama's boy," Dante says, his voice choked up.

"It's alright," Will says with a shrug, then adds, "You did get one thing right."

"What's that?" Dante asks, tipping his chin.

"I am a nerd. And proud of it!" Will says, and they both laugh, then put on their headsets and stomp their feet as they start to play.

On the field, Tabeen drives the ball into Victorian territory. She passes it to Avery. I tap and start recording a video of her racing toward their goal. Georgia, instead of calling for the ball, blocks Marta and gives Avery a chance to kick on goal. Jaguars score!

"*Woohoo!*" Cora and I jump up. I post the video, tagging Georgia and Avery. #CutestKickEver. Georgia's mom waves her rhinestone cap as Coach Hartley shouts, "Way to go, team!"

A part of me misses playing goalie. Maybe next year I'll join the team again, but for now I'm perfectly content.

Glossary

3-D printing: Is a special kind of printer to make things out of plastic or other materials. Instead of printing on paper though, it builds up layers of the material to make a 3-dimensional object. It's a bit like using a glue gun to make a sculpture out of plastic, but the printer can make much more detailed and complex shapes. It's like magic! You can take a design on a computer and "print" it into a real object you can hold in your hand.

AI: Stands for **Artificial Intelligence**. It's like a computer brain that can think and learn on its own, without being told what to do. It's a way to make computers and machines more like humans. There are different types of AI, like ones that can recognize faces or understand what people are saying, and others that can play games or drive cars. It's pretty cool, because it can make things easier and more efficient for us.

But just like any other technology, AI has some potential dangers. One of the dangers of AI is that it can make mistakes, and some of those mistakes can have big consequences. For example, if an AI system controls a car, and it makes a mistake, it could cause an accident. Another danger of AI is that it can be used for bad things, like hacking into computers or spreading fake information.

Biomimicry: Is when people look at nature and use the ideas and designs they find there to make new things. It's like copying what works well in nature to make our own things work better. For example, scientists might look at the way a bird's wing is shaped and use that design to make a more efficient airplane wing. Or, engineers might look at the way a shark's skin is rough on one side and smooth on the other, and use that idea to make a boat that moves through water more quickly.

Echolocation: Is like a superpower that some animals have. They make a special sound, like a chirp or a click, and then they listen to the echoes that come back. By listening to these echoes, they can tell where things are around them, even in the dark or in murky water. It's a bit like playing a game of "Marco Polo" but instead of saying the words, the animals make sounds and listen for the echoes. Some animals like bats and dolphins use echolocation to navigate and hunt for food. It's pretty cool!

Electrolytes: Special chemicals that help your body work properly. They are kind of like little helpers that are found in your blood and other fluids in your body. They help your muscles move and your nerves work correctly. Electrolytes also help balance the fluids in your body, so you don't get dehydrated. They are like little batteries that help your body's electrical system run smoothly. You can find electrolytes in things like sports drinks, or you can get them from eating certain foods like fruits and vegetables.

Electromagnetic Spectrum: Is a big term for all the different types of energy that travel through space. Imagine a rainbow, with all different colors of the rainbow, each color of the rainbow represents a different type of energy. Each color is a different type of energy, like radio waves, microwaves, infrared, visible light, ultraviolet, X-rays and Gamma rays. Each type of energy is used for different things like microwaves that help cook our food, visible light helps us see, ultraviolet helps us make vitamin D, and X-rays help doctors see inside our bodies.

Hackathon: An event where people come together to use their computer skills to create something new and exciting. Imagine a big party where instead of dancing and playing games, everyone is sitting at computers and working on a project. These projects can be anything from building a new app, to creating a website, to designing a new piece of technology. It's a fun and creative way to learn, experiment, and develop solutions to real-world problems, with the help of a community of like-minded individuals. It's a great opportunity for kids to learn new skills and collaborate with other kids who share the same interests, and to showcase their creativity and problem-solving abilities.

Loophole: A computer loophole is a way for someone to use a computer or technology to do something that is not allowed or is harmful. Just like a loophole in a rule or law, it's a sneaky way to get around something that is supposed to be protected. For example, imagine a computer program that is supposed to keep your personal information private, but there's a way to get into that program and see your information without permission. That's called a computer loophole. It's important to know that computer loopholes can be used by people with bad intentions and it's important to protect yourself and your information by being aware of them and taking necessary precautions.

Magnets: Objects that can attract or repel certain metals, like iron or steel. They have north and south poles, and opposite poles are attracted to each other while the same poles will push away from each other. Some common examples of magnets are the ones you might use on your refrigerator to hold up pictures or notes. Magnets can also be found in things like electric motors and speakers..

Microbes: Tiny living things that you can't see with your eyes. They are too small to be seen without a microscope. Microbes can be bacteria, viruses, and other microorganisms. Some of them are good for you and help your body to work properly. Others can make you sick and cause infections. They are everywhere, in the air, water, soil, and even on our skin and in our gut. Some of them can be beneficial for us, like the ones that help us digest food, and some can be harmful, like the ones that cause diseases.

Probiotics: Tiny microbes, like germs or bacteria, that are good for your body. They live in your gut and help you digest food and stay healthy. Think of them like microscopic helpers that live inside you and keep your stomach and intestines working properly.

Migration: When animals or people move from one place to another, usually because of changes in weather or for food. Just like how birds fly south for the winter, or salmon swim upstream to lay their eggs.

Nitrogen: A gas that makes up most of the air we breathe. Plants and animals need nitrogen to survive, because it's a key ingredient in making proteins, which help them grow and stay healthy. Some farmers use nitrogen to make their crops grow bigger and better, just like how you would add water and sunlight to help a flower grow.

VR: Stands for **Virtual Reality**. It's like a computer game, but instead of just looking at the screen, you wear a special headset that covers your eyes and ears. The headset makes it feel like you are inside the game, like you are really there. You can look around, move your head, and even walk around in the virtual world. It's like being in a dream, but you can control what you see and do.

Acknowledgements

I am so grateful to my family and friends for supporting me through the birth of this story. The inspiration for KyRose came from my sister Ipek Serifsoy who gave me the courage to create a heroine to inspire our daughters—Melise and Sema—beyond fairytale princesses. I have endless gratitude for my mother Ayla Etizsoy Serifsoy (ever the artist, even at the age of 84) for highlighting nature and animals and showing me how to create art at an early age which ignited the maker/tinkerer in me, along with my father Atagun Serifsoy who taught me how to think like an engineer.

I'm blessed by my amazing children Melise and Destin who opened the door I had shut years ago (to cope with the rigors of work-life) so I may once again reconnect with my inner child and see the world harmoniously.

Thank you to Al Watt, the best writing teacher in the world, who provided me with structure and a community of writers, and who faithfully guided me to uncover the story within me.

In doing research for the concepts in this book, I came across the works of many scientists, engineers, authors, and psychologists who inspired and informed me. I'm grateful for their ingenuity and curiosity. Special thanks to Janine M. Benyus, David Eagleman, Jane Goodall, Rachel Carson, Peter Diamandis, Sir Ken Robinson, Ed Yong, David Suzuki, Rosalind Wiseman, and Daniel J. Siegel.

When it came time to editing and the final

presentation of the book, it certainly took a team. Many thanks to Jessica McKelden for final copy editing, to Mariya Prytula for the beautiful cover and interior book design, to Victor Kyalo for multiple rounds of formatting, and to my daughter Melise for all her playful artwork on the chapter headings.

Thank you, Samantha and Lucas Posell for sharing your expertise on soccer plays. And, thank you to my dear friend Peri Doslu who helped me name my character KyRose, capturing the essence of the ancient Greek god Kairos. I'm blessed by my community of loving friends who cheered me along over the years as I wrote this story. Special thanks to Astrid Oviedo Clark, Fiona Posell, Zanne Devine, Jane Akdoruk and her son Henry Brown who read early versions of the book and gave me valuable feedback. And, big heartfelt thanks to all my friends on my launch team who are helping spread-the-word to bring this novel into the hands of young readers.

Drum roll. Last, but least, I wholeheartedly, thank my brilliant, loving husband Paul Bricault who read countless drafts and supported me over the years as I pursued this dream until it became a reality. Muah!

About the Author

Cicek Bricault is passionate about living in balance with nature. She hopes to inspire youngsters and adults to follow their passions—and to use technology to problem solve and safe guard the delicate ecosystems on our planet. She tries to live slowly…and drop into *The Zone* like the ancient Greek god Kairos, which was the inspiration for her heroine KyRose.

Cicek (pronounced *Chee-check*) lives in Venice Beach, California with her husband, daughter, son, mother and their dog Bogie. They love to watch the sunsets on their green roof. Cicek is currently working on a podcast for Crafty Makers and loves to wander the globe to speak with remarkable creators and innovators of all ages. Meet her on Instagram @KyRoseLoves and visit www.KyRoseLoves.com for her favorite maker projects that your whole family can enjoy.

Reading Group Guide
By Cicek Bricault

1. KyRose joins the soccer team to be friends with Georgia in the hopes of getting invited to her next party. Yet, when Georgia recruits her on the team (p. 5) KyRose hesitates because she's scared she won't be good enough. What clue does this give us into KyRose's personality?

2. Have you ever wanted something but felt scared to go for it? KyRose tries to convince Cora to join the soccer team (p. 15) so Cora will get invited to Georgia's party too, but could KyRose have another reason for Cora to be on the team? How does Cora comfort her when she asks "But what if I mess up?"

3. The Think-It device advertised on the refrigerator screen in KyRose's kitchen (p. 30) links directly to people's brains with wires and implants. Sounds great, right? But, Dad's eyes bulge with fear of a hacker gaining control. If this was an invention in real life (and it just might be, look up Neuralink), what good could come of it? And, what bad? Give examples of the ideas you have.

4. When the GoMars project is announced and Cora humiliates Georgia in front of the class and says "I'm not your slave, you know," what decision does KyRose make afterwards. How does this change (the level of honesty in) her friendship with Cora, and her honesty with herself?

5. When Will takes Dante's dare to jump off Georgia's roof into her pool (p. 152) he shouts "I'm not scared!" loud enough for everyone to hear. Why does Will care so much about people think about him? Do you think the secret guilt he feels about his mother's death adds to him trying to keep a tough exterior? How do the dangers he faces under water in chapter 24 and admitting he was scared set him free. What does Will learn by the end of the story that sets him free?

6. KyRose tells her teammates about the "*The Zone*" (p. 82). Can you give an example of when time slowed and you felt like you were in *The Zone*? Maybe when doing a puzzle or drawing a picture.

7. KyRose loses her power to speak to animals when she turns her back on Misty (p. 190). What happens on the beach (p. 214) that allows her powers to return?

8. Animal intelligence plays a key role in the book. Can you cite examples like the viper that can see in the dark with heat sensors and sea turtles that use the earth's magnetic field to navigate? If you could pick a superpower, what would it be? And, how would you use it to solve a problem and make the world a better place?

9. Rebecca loves to sing, yet (like KyRose) she gives her power away and turns her back on her dreams so she can fit in with the Primas. How does being in *The Zone* help Rebecca to realize how important her dreams are to her?

10. Sarafina is KyRose's virtual AI assistant. Do you have an AI assistant? It could be Siri, Alexa, or another software. What kinds of questions do you ask it? What other questions and jobs do you wish it could answer and do for you?

11. Would you like to join The Buster Club? If so, what mysteries and crimes against nature and animals would you want to solve?

The Story Goes On

In book two of this trilogy, KyRose and The Buster Club race to solve a mystery around Kew Gardens in London, England. These gardens house one of the largest *seed* banks in the world. The seeds are from a variety of plants across the globe and have been collected by explorers and scientist over hundreds of years. The bank ensures that if a plant goes extinct, its seed will be tucked away safely so we can grow the plant and bring the species back to life. But, something's gone awry, and the seed bank is in jeopardy. Can KyRose and her friends help save the day?

Stay tuned.

Visit www.KyRoseLoves.com to join our community and receive updates on books and STEAM activities that empower kids, teachers and parents everywhere.

Made in the USA
Las Vegas, NV
12 February 2023